Mapping Discipleship is a   guide for Christian growth grounded in Scripture. Carter effectively addresses the call to personal sanctification with the need for a clear, biblical framework for discipleship. His approach is theologically sound and deeply practical, providing valuable insights for believers seeking to walk faithfully in their calling. This book will be helpful for Christians seeking to grow in Christ or those who are discipling others.

Scott Aniol
Executive Vice President, G3 Ministries

Christ's commission to make disciples of all nations culminates with "teaching them to observe all that I have commanded you." In Mapping Discipleship, Charlie rightly emphasizes the believer's need to know the truth of the Word and to live the truth of the Word. We can't live the Word if we don't know it, but knowing it without living it produces self-deception, not Christlikeness. Charlie guides us on a path of connecting the Word to life through a series of 12 questions and responses that remind us of the authority of Christ in our lives, of the presence of His Spirit in us, and of the reality that God blends the blessings and burdens of our lives together in His providential care for us, moving us toward the character of Christ. Our response to this loving work of God: submit our desires to the work of the Spirit through the Word. The outcome: the glory of God is reflected in our lives as the light of Christ's character is seen in us. The time you spend reading this book will refocus you on God's central purpose in life, assist you in realigning your heart to that purpose, and provide you with real hope that you can live out His purpose. Along the way, Charlie will help you to rightly define and desire true discipleship relationships.

Jeff Newman
Administrator for Safe Haven for Missionary Soul Care, Baptist
Mid-Missions

Discipleship is an indispensable but often ill-defined ministry in the lives of Christians and the church. The confusion around the topic has left many feeling like they are spinning their wheels, stuck in a rut, or walking in circles. Charlie Carter has given clarity to the church with this simple, usable, yet rich atlas to God's means of transformation in the life of believers. Whether used individually to gain insight into God's sanctifying grace or (better) used with another, *Mapping Discipleship* guides the reader on a journey that will be truly breathtaking in its glory.

Jeff Dilyard
Pastor, Pleasant Hill Baptist Church, Smithville, OH

In *Mapping Discipleship*, Charlie Carter provides followers of Christ with an incredibly helpful guidebook for the discipleship journey. Using the metaphor of a map, he explains with plenty of wit and creativity what discipleship is and how God transforms believers into the image of Christ. Carter does not reduce discipleship to a trite method. Instead, he develops the rich biblical-theological relationship between discipleship and sanctification. I am thankful for this valuable contribution to the church and look forward to using *Mapping Discipleship* in my ministry.

Doug Brown
Seminary Dean, Faith Baptist Theological Seminary, Ankeny, IA

We often seek the path of least resistance, but this book maps out a course of spiritual growth that navigates the realities of life rather than bypassing them. Even better, Carter reveals how testing and trials become effective means of reaching the destination of inner renewal through transformative training and walking in the Spirit. Fellow travelers along the road of discipleship will appreciate the biblical and practical insights of this faithful guide.

Paul Hartog
Senior Professor, Faith Baptist Theological Seminary, Ankeny, IA

In *Mapping Discipleship*, Charlie Carter gives concrete, genuine hope—you can be different; you can grow. Using 12 questions, *Mapping Discipleship* clearly sets out the goal and method of discipleship in such understandable language and pleasant writing that every Christian can benefit. *Mapping Discipleship* won't let a Christian settle for outward conformity; rather, Carter pushes change at the heart level. He gives attainable metrics, memorable illustrations, and concrete direction to encourage hope-filled discipleship. His biblical view of growth is encouraging by being simple, straightforward, and realistic. Carter's metaphors and illustrations are as on target as they are challenging. No Christian will be unsure or confused about the next steps after reading *Mapping Discipleship*.

Kraig Keck
Lead Pastor, First Baptist Church, Colville, WA

Charlie Carter's perspective on the often misunderstood concept of discipleship brings clarity and insight. He combines biblical wisdom with practical guidance, offering actionable steps to help any Christian deepen their faith while better supporting others. I highly recommend this book to anyone looking for personal growth or seeking to assist others in their spiritual development.

Dave Callison
Assistant Director, Iowa Regular Baptist Camp, Ventura, IA

MAPPING DISC IPLE SHIP

12 QUESTIONS FOR NAVIGATING TRIALS ON THE ROAD TO TRANSFORMATION

CHARLIE CARTER

Print ISBN: 978-1-960820-07-5
Digital ISBN: 978-1-960820-08-2

Library of Congress Control Number: 2024921242

Front cover image and book design by Lance Young with Higher Rock Creative Studio

Faith Publications
1900 NW 4th St.
Ankeny, IA 50023

faith.edu/publications

Printed in the United States of America
All rights reserved

15 14 13 12 11 10 9 8 7 6 5 4 3 2 1

THIS BOOK IS DEDICATED TO

THE CHURCH
& THINKLINGS
EVERYWHERE.

TABLE OF CONTENTS

ACKNOWLEDGMENTS

Harvest Baptist Church, Open Door Baptist Church, and Maranatha Baptist Church are my spiritual beginnings as well as past and present ministry homes. I would have nothing to say about the spiritual life without you. Any length of words is an understatement of my thankfulness to you all. I love you each more than you know.

Iowa Regular Baptist Camp & Faith Baptist Bible College have too much influence to recognize truly. Thank you for forming me theologically and cultivating a heart for ministry.

Blue Cow, I would not have finished this book without you. Thank you, Andrew, Joey, Logan, Chase, and the friendliest herd around.

Brickhouse Coffee Co. & Porch Light Coffee House, I wrote this book at your tables. I could not have done this without brew.

John S, Lance A, Tim J, Brandon F, Ryan S, Ryan K, Mark S, Jordan S, Dirk Z, Bill B, Steve J, Justin L, Dr. Newman, Dr. Cole, Dr. Ken, Dr. Doug, Dr. Dan, Dr. Paul, and Dr. Myron, thank you for being my spiritual, theological, and ministry mentors & friends.

Jeff, Seth, Joe, Max, Luke, Sam, Noah, Jason, Lance, Jacob, Drew, Jason, Alex, Christian, Dalton, David, Cole, Ethan, Carter, Asa, and Sawyer, thank you for allowing me to be a part of your discipleship journey. There are many others I could mention, not the least being each of my students. You are all loved.

Thank you, Cameron, Jonathon, Paul, Tim, Andy, and Josh, for being fellow hobbits who have gone there with me and would go back again if I asked.

Last but not least, thank you, Dad, Mom, and Michael, for all your love.

Foreword to Mapping Discipleship

The apostle Paul wrote, "But know this, that in the last days perilous times will come: for men will be lovers of themselves, . . . having a form of godliness but denying its power. . . . Always learning and never able to come to the knowledge of the truth" (2 Tim 3:1–7 NKJV).[1] Despite our living in a time with increasing resources for a knowledge of the truth, it appears that a diminishing number of believers are truly being transformed by the grace of the glory of the gospel (2 Cor 3:16–18). As we believers are perplexed by this dilemma, we are compelled to ask, Why is this happening? It seems certain that the world is on a steep trajectory of moral decline, similar to that of Lot's days in Sodom and Gomorrah.

Peter explains that Lot "was oppressed by the filthy conduct of the wicked (for that righteous man, dwelling among them, tormented his righteous soul from day to day by seeing and hearing their lawless deeds)" and that "the Lord knows how to deliver the godly out of temptations and to reserve the unjust under punishment for the day of judgment" (2 Pet 2:7–9). Despite what is at work in the world, we can find hope in these words and in the Lord, who knows how to deliver the godly out of every trial. We must come to understand the wisdom of the way He works within us (1) to will and to do for His good pleasure (Phil 2:13) and (2) to

---

1 All Scripture quotations in this foreword are from the NKJV.

preserve us in the light of the glory of the gospel (2 Cor 4:7). As followers of Christ, we must be able to answer the question, How is God at work in my life right now? In the pages that follow, Charlie will show you from the Bible how God desires to work in the heart and life of every believer.

How should we stand strong in the wisdom of the ways of God and the power of the glory of the gospel? Paul testifies of this in 2 Corinthians 4:6–7, "For it is God who commanded the light to shine out of darkness, who has shone in our hearts to give the light of the glory of God in the face of Jesus Christ. But we have this treasure in earthen vessels that the power may be of God and not of us." Let us be light shining in darkness, holding fast and holding forth the Word of truth! Paul reminds us, "Not that we are sufficient of ourselves to think of anything as being from ourselves, but our sufficiency is from God" (2 Cor 3:5).

In the same context of 2 Timothy 3, where Paul warns against future peril and having a form of godliness without the power, we notice that he also commends Timothy, "But you have carefully followed my doctrine, manner of life, purpose, faith, longsuffering, love, perseverance, persecutions, afflictions, which happened to me." We must ask ourselves, Could that commendation be said of me? Or is there a gap between our comprehension and our application of the knowledge of our Lord and His gospel? Is something lacking in the teaching and training process of our discipleship that contributes to this deficiency? Make it your prayer to share the heart of Moses: "If I have found grace in Your sight, show me now Your way, that I may know You" (Exod 33:13).

Spiritual training involves what Paul referred to: our manner of life, purpose, faith, even our perseverance during persecutions and afflictions—afflictions or pressures that occur under the Lord's leading and sovereign hand. The Lord tests each of us, to humble us and cause us to look inward and upward: inward to see what is in our hearts; then, as we learn of the sin in our hearts, upward in dependence on Him.

We find an example of the Lord doing this very thing in John 6, during the feeding of the five thousand. Jesus said to Philip, "Where shall we buy bread, that these may eat? But this He said to test him, for He Himself knew what He would do" (vv. 5–6). Is there something significant in the way the Lord was directing the disciples' steps, in the purpose He desired to accomplish within them? What is that significance? What is that purpose? The answers to these questions and the ones Charlie presents in this book are vital for our spiritual growth. It is my prayer that after reading this book, you will marvel at the wisdom of the way in which the Lord works within us both to will and to do for His good pleasure! I am grateful to Charlie for undertaking the task of communicating such valuable insights into the wisdom of the ways of God. May it give you greater clarity in understanding how the Lord works within us to accomplish His purposes for His glory, "to give the light of the knowledge of the glory of God in the face of Jesus Christ" (2 Cor 4:6)! May the Lord bless the teaching and truth of His Word to the training of your heart and life.

John Sauser
Pastor, Harvest Baptist Church, Williamsburg, Iowa

Author's Preface

God has a plan to change His people, always including good questions. From God asking Adam and Eve, "Where are you?" to Jesus asking the twelve, "Who do you say that I am?" God has employed questions to spiritually challenge His followers and cultivate their hearts to fear and love Him more. God uses questions to make disciples.

Effective disciple-makers today should also utilize well-crafted questions in their discipleship relationships. Parents, pastors, preachers, church leaders, mentors, or anyone seeking to make disciples should learn to ask good questions. Discipleship involves knowing the answers to difficult questions and applying that knowledge wisely.

Wisdom

Any discipleship that neglects the fear or love of God runs astray. Genuine, lasting discipleship begins in the heart as disciples' loves, desires, and motives transform to resemble Jesus. The task of discipleship looks no different in any location—successful discipleship stresses internal transformation.

Most believers willingly sign up to follow Jesus but reconsider when difficulties arrive. Many love to quote the warm, fuzzy sayings of Jesus but, unfortunately, forget that he promised trial, temptation, and suffering in earthly life. Everyone loves comfort, and Christians are no exception. One problem: if believers skip the trial, they also skip the transformation. Trials will not magically disappear after conversion, and sinful human nature continues to war and fight with God's Spirit within each believer. Each Christian today desperately needs to learn and live a life controlled by the Holy Spirit through the Word of God.

TRIALS

Trials do not hinder transformation; they lead us further down the road of progressive change. Many people want discipleship to be a clean, comfortable list of tasks: go to church, read the Bible, pray, etc. Those activities help the process, but authentic discipleship happens as tests prompt a genuine walk in wisdom; authentic discipleship trains believers to answer the right questions about themselves and their hearts during pressure.

This book compiles and distills thousands of one-on-one discipleship meetings. Each chapter includes a question the Lord and the Word ask us to consider in our trials of life. When I was sixteen and a brand-new Christian, my pastor asked me some of these. I have added observations, implications, and conclusions from theology professors, mentors, and years of pastoral and practical ministry. These chapters encompass hundreds of lengthy meetings, awkward silences, wordy discussions, and tearful prayers with believers at camps, colleges, and churches.

God blessed me with the mentors who discipled me and the blessing to disciple others. Despite my sin and insufficiency, I have watched God transform many—beginning with myself. This book shares a philosophy and method that leads to successful discipleship. Like an old trowel, may this book be plunged into the soil year after year as new seeds are planted. Trowels do nothing flashy or exciting but significantly help cultivate the soil for gardeners who like to get their hands dirty. I hope this book is your discipleship trowel. In your home, church, and realms of spiritual influence, may you grow and seek to train disciples to live out the gospel effectively.

You're Going on an Adventure: Here's a Map

People today carry a GPS in their pockets; it directs them wherever they want to go. The contrarian in me heavily prefers maps. While in college, I traveled a few summers on a team that visited Bible camps and churches around the United States. During one of those summers, my copilot, Joey, and I decided to travel old school. We purchased a large book of maps to help us navigate the different cities and locations in the itinerary. Although we had smartphones, maps provided such a better experience.

A good map benefits an adventuring explorer, but the map never substitutes for any actual exploring. Maps of Phoenix and Omaha helped Joey and me reach specific destinations; but when we arrived, we put the map down, jumped out of the vehicle, and began to explore. Even though the maps got us to those places, our stories are about much more than maps. Alister McGrath applies a map analogy to theological creeds in *Mere Discipleship*, saying, "A map cannot even begin to convey the vibrant colors, rich textures, and subtle fragrances of a glorious landscape. It cannot tell us what it is like to live there. Nor is a mere diagram on a piece of paper going to do justice to the beauty and majesty of the natural world. *But it is not meant to.*"[1] Maps get us where we need to go, but we Christians must go where no geographical map can take us.

As McGrath observed regarding theology, sometimes maps are helpful when exploring unseen places, which exist in the imagination or creativity of the mind. As an example, Middle-earth is the imaginary land in *The Lord of the Rings*, in which Frodo, Sam, Gandalf, and Gimli live. Though Middle-earth may not be physically real, Tolkien's maps help his readers explore intangible locations like the Shire, Gondor, and Mordor. Trading Middle-earth for the "land" of discipleship, *Mapping Discipleship* helps disciples explore the land's significant stops.

This book maps out the land of discipleship, and, like a map, will guide you to prominent ideas but will never substitute for your own exploring, cultivating, and living. The three main destinations along the road of discipleship are *recognition, response, and reflection*. Each of these major stops includes a few minor destinations, expressed through questions that serve as lampposts shedding increasing light upon the path as you travel through the major ports, cities, and terrain in the land of discipleship. To the extent that the questions help you consider and wisely apply Scripture, this map will land you in green pastures and beside still waters.

Each question includes Bible passages to study, further questions to prompt thinking and reflection, practical steps for application, and theological considerations. The questions serve as a teaching method. The further you walk down the road to each destination, the more vivid and memorable your stay will be. But avoid getting bogged down by one question too long. The land is vast; keep walking.

This book will also help you learn the "lay of the land" well enough to commit and train other disciples. You should eventually

1   Alister McGrath, *Mere Discipleship* (Grand Rapids, MI: Baker Books, 2018), 23. My emphasis added.

become a tour guide, using this book to guide others. Even as a guide, you yourself should never stop exploring, but you will walk others down the challenging and beautiful road of discipleship. This book is my attempt to show you some of the beautiful places I have found.

With these things in mind, I want to provide a "key" to the map. The rest of this introduction unfolds a few working definitions and explanations related to discipleship and the method of this book. As with any of the chapters, I hope you do not get too bogged down with the rest of the introduction. If you find that happening, just run to the next stop. You can always backtrack and complete the introduction later.

A Key to the Map: What Is Discipleship?

The idea of discipleship persists in the language of most Christian churches, schools, and communities, but many Christians easily misunderstand the term *discipleship* and its derivatives. An inability to answer What is discipleship? threatens the journey before it begins. Definitions drive methodology, so starting with a definition will assist us in successfully exploring discipleship. The following four discipleship terms deserve specific attention: *disciple, disciple-maker, discipleship,* and *Christian discipleship.*

A disciple is simply a learner. A disciple-maker, then, would be a creator/crafter of learners. We commonly call these people teachers. Teachers can teach formally, with lectures, notes, etc., or by example and experience. Similarly, learners learn both intellectually and practically. Either way, a disciple is a learner, and a disciple-maker is a teacher.

Discipleship, broadly, refers to some association of the learner and teacher: they participate together in the process of discipleship, both hold responsibilities, and both have goals to accomplish. A well-balanced definition of *discipleship* specifies the collaboration of disciples and disciple-makers, describing their roles and relationships. Here is my attempt: *Discipleship is the fellowship of a teacher and learner in which a disciple-maker guides the disciple in acquiring knowledge and applying it to life.*

Discipleship between teachers and learners exists outside of Christianity. Most trades utilize apprenticeship and mentorship, which require no Christian theology. For example, mechanics usually learn to fix cars from other mechanics. An apprentice mechanic obtains knowledge and skills to repair vehicles by following the teaching and example of an experienced mechanic. Similar relationships between professional teachers and new learners occur throughout many professions and trades. Teachers teach, and learners learn. That's discipleship.

What is the difference between discipleship of a mechanic, for example, and discipleship in the Christian life? Christian disciples must be Christians; the teaching and the learning occur between two church members who believe in the gospel. The best location for Christian discipleship is (and will always be) the local church. Christian discipleship also happens within families and homes united in the doctrine and unity of a local church.

Further, Christian discipleship includes unique content (teaching), goals (transformation), and means (training). Christian discipleship focuses on people rather than on inanimate things—more specifically, it targets a person's immaterial dimension for transformation. Christian discipleship also focuses on glorifying God through a believer's Christlike character. The method for discipleship—spiritual training through trials—also differs from the method of the mechanic. These three areas—teaching, transformation, and training—are broad categories to consider in discipleship.

Teaching: Understanding and Applying the Words of Jesus

Christian discipleship features distinct content and a focus on following Jesus. We learn to follow Jesus through the written word of God. So, following Jesus requires acquiring and knowing the doctrines of Christianity and learning the distinctions between biblical and false teaching. A Christian disciple commits to learning the revelation of God, its interpretation, and its application to daily living.

Teaching the Bible forms part of Jesus's command in Matthew 28:18–20. Often referred to as the Great Commission, Jesus's commission specifically identifies His own words as the content of discipleship: "Go, therefore, and make disciples of all nations, baptizing them in the name of the Father, Son, and Holy Spirit, *teaching them to observe all things I have commanded you.*"

Christian discipleship, therefore, teaches the commands of Jesus and the whole counsel of God. The Old Testament Law, Prophets, and other writings and the New Testament Gospels and Epistles encapsulate the content of Christian discipleship. This book—this "map"—helps readers explore the Bible, but not comprehensively.

Second Timothy 2:1–7 is another New Testament passage that guides us regarding the content of discipleship. In these verses, the apostle Paul encourages Timothy to instruct others with the same teaching that Timothy had received from Paul: "*What you have heard* from me in the presence of many witnesses . . . entrust to faithful men . . . who will be able to teach others also."

Paul, a prime example of a disciple-maker, discipled Timothy by teaching him the word of God. The primary message in Paul's teaching was the gospel of Jesus: that Jesus died for the world's sins, was buried, and rose again from the dead. The gospel and its ramifications to daily life will always provide abundant discipleship content. The gospel is the beginning with no end, and Christians continue learning the greater depth and beauty of the death, burial, and resurrection of Jesus.

Paul's teaching also included the grace that Jesus desires for the church. Paul both wrote these teachings in his letters to Timothy, and instructed Timothy directly during their extensive missionary endeavors together. Further, Paul expected Timothy to disciple others by following his example: teaching the doctrines of the Christian faith and the way to live by them.

As Jesus and Paul demonstrate, the content of Christian discipleship remains the word of God. So, anyone wanting to explore discipleship must cultivate a love for Scripture. Christian discipleship includes more than mere intellectual recall or assent. For the goal of Christian discipleship involves the Christian's mind, heart, and will. God's will is for wholistic transformation.

Transformation: Obedience Resulting from Changed Character

The results of Christian discipleship differ drastically from any other mentorship or training. And proper learning the word of God encompasses more than passing a theology test. The road of discipleship travels beyond mere knowledge and voyages deep into a person's heart. God seeks to transform each disciple internally. Consider a few of Jesus's teachings in the Sermon on the Mount:

> You have heard that it was said to those of old, "You shall not murder; and whoever murders will be liable to judgment." But I say to you that everyone who is angry with his brother will be liable to judgment; whoever insults his brother will be liable to the council; and whoever says, "You fool!" will be liable to the hell of fire. (Matt 5:21)

> You have heard that it was said, "You shall not commit adultery." But I say to you that everyone who looks at a woman with lustful intent has already committed adultery with her in his heart. (Matt 5:27)

Murder and adultery are unholy, so obedience necessitates abstaining from killing and sexual immorality. However, each of these commands possesses an internal component. Jesus commands and expects internal holiness. External conformity to the law is insufficient for a person to be holy. So, Jesus calls attention to the desires and motives of the heart.

Yes, murder is a sin, but what about anger? Anger originates internally and extends externally. Adultery is also a sin, but so is lust in the heart. Jesus's teaching demands internal awareness and a change of character. Christians describe this internal process with multiple words: *growing, being sanctified, changing, maturing,* and the like. All these words refer to the process of internal, spiritual transformation. Spiritual transformation is the goal of Christian discipleship: a disciple learns to act as Jesus would as that person's heart changes to love what Jesus loves.

All disciples acquire knowledge, but only Christian disciples need genuine character transformation. A mechanic needs specific knowledge to fix a car, but a carburetor does not care about character. An honest mechanic might be preferred, but fixing cars does not require virtue. An older mechanic achieves discipleship success when the new mechanic knows how to fix a car. But a Christian disciple-maker succeeds only when the Christian disciple learns the doctrines of the word of God, and those teachings transform that disciple.

These two dimensions of Christian discipleship—knowledge acquisition of God's word and genuine character transformation— provide the bookends of discipleship. A disciple-maker teaches the word of God to another disciple with the goal of spiritual transformation. Knowing the end destination helps us begin the journey, but a clear path forward is always helpful. So, does a path exist for the disciple-maker and disciple to walk together to seek the knowledge and character required in Christian discipleship? Or let me ask it a different way: *How* does spiritual transformation happen through teaching?

Training: The Path to Successful Christian Discipleship

Unfortunately, transformation through teaching eludes many in Christian discipleship. Most disciple-makers search for external markers of Christian growth and use these external markers to determine success. Thus, evangelism, Bible reading, Bible memory, church attendance, church service, following the Ten Commandments, etc., become the measurement of successful discipleship. These are suitable tasks, and each should be encouraged in the church. However, the aim of Christian discipleship is not task completion but character transformation. This target proves more difficult to hit than the typical list of external Christian standards.

Pastors, Bible camps, collegiate ministries, and parents all seek visible evidence to determine successful discipleship. Using the activities listed above to indicate success is not wrong, and disciple-makers expect external fruits like Bible reading, evangelism, and obedience to be present and growing in the life of a disciple. However, though fruits are helpful, disciple-makers must understand that external fruits can be misleading.

External behaviors do not prove that spiritual growth is taking place. *It is possible to adopt certain behaviors and fool people into thinking that our external behavior results from transformed character.* Many people, for example, buy fruit at a store but never grow it personally. Christian discipleship, on the other hand, succeeds only when disciples grow their own fruit.

If external tasks equal discipleship success, a disciple-maker only needs a methodology for these tasks. Discipleship then becomes behaviorism. Imagine a car with a beautiful exterior that won't start or run. If our goal is to drive, we need gas in the tank and a running car! Who cares what the car looks like? The temptation persists to create disciples who focus on external tasks and neglect spiritual transformation. Ideally, external change and internal change are in concert with each other. While external tasks often provide opportunities for transformation, tasks are not an end in themselves. A disciple-maker therefore needs a methodology to train disciples in the details of character transformation.

How does a disciple-maker help a disciple reach genuine character transformation? What should parents do when a child conforms to external standards but may not have changing affections within the heart? When a pastor, counselor, or friend watches someone take all the proper external steps but suspects the person is just going through the motions, what should that pastor, counselor, or friend do? Jesus faced similar issues with His disciple-making, and his answer emphasized the internal component of discipleship. Jesus reinforced the connection between external behaviors and the heart.

Again, Jesus's words in the Sermon on the Mount clarify this internal emphasis. Murder is wrong but so is anger; adultery is wrong but so is lust in the heart. True obedience requires changed hearts. Further, the theme of transformed inner desire has always been the foundation of biblical wisdom and is represented well in the Old Testament:

"Love the LORD your God with *all your heart*" (Deut 6:5).
"*The fear of the LORD* is the beginning of wisdom" (Prov 9:10).

Loving and fearing God with the heart necessitates a change of the heart, that is, genuine character transformation. Like natural fruit sprouting from its roots, spiritual fruit proceeds from the heart. Jesus modeled this perfect love of the Father, internally and externally, and disciples today follow his example. Christian disciples need to be like Christ. *The process of discipleship is learning to love what Jesus loves and transforming to be like Him, beginning in the heart, extending to our actions, and multiplying through teaching others.* Jesus's example and teaching provide the path to spiritual transformation.

Jesus promised suffering, and the successful discipleship path involves suffering to glorify Christ. Those willing to walk this path are directed daily by the heavenly Father as His children, so we do not walk this path of spiritual training alone. The rest of this book explores this path, with the guiding question, What is successful discipleship?

Welcome to the land of discipleship! The following twelve stops on the road offer wonderful exploration for all disciples and disciple-makers. Learn the local knowledge and acquire a love for the local flavor. Your stay may last longer in specific locations than others. I encourage all disciples to walk the path before running. You cannot fly to the end; do not be hasty. Arriving at transformation takes time. At many points, you may, rightfully, diverge into other theological fields or practical pastures—I encourage you to do this. I trust God will bless the study of his word, the goal of discipleship in the church, and your pursuit of Christ-like character.

RECOGNIZE

VIEWING GOD'S WILL
AS INTERNAL CHANGE

What Is God's Will?

People who love assembling puzzles generally start with the border. Straightedge pieces can be quickly gathered and easily connected, since they have fewer sides to match. The outside serves as a guide, leading construction of the puzzle in a straightforward progression from the outer edges toward the center. It would seem absurd for someone to begin solving a puzzle from the inside. Why waste time and energy? The most efficient method is to start from the outside.

Similarly, most people focus on fixing the outside when solving life's puzzles. Difficult people and circumstances complicate life, and many individuals attempt to solve their challenging situations by reconstructing or rearranging their physical lives. They believe that by changing their location, job, marital status, or material possessions, they can quickly solve life's puzzles. But is seeking a comfortable home, stable employment, a loving spouse, or material wealth the solution?

Solving the Puzzle of God's Will Is Possible

Christians might approach finding God's will in the same way. They desire to know what the future holds, and they view God's will as a destination to reach or a crucial decision. They believe making the right choice will accurately reflect God's desires and lead them to a "good life." They see God's will as merely a skill—mastering the art of decision-making. Although making right choices is important, God desires to transform far more than just the corner and edge pieces of our lives.

Authentic wisdom results from an internal transformation rather than from the sum of individual decisions, important though they may be. Making a wise choice requires a change in our thinking and emotions. Wisdom begins on the inside, not the outside. So, while we believers prioritize wisdom as a destination, we must also walk the right path to acquire it. And although God's will encompasses both destination and path, the beginning of the journey lies within the human heart. It might sound counterintuitive, but we solve the puzzle of God's will from the inside, not the outside.

God's Will Is Internal Transformation

The process of internal transformation begins with salvation. Ephesians 2:1 clearly states that we are all spiritually dead due to sin, but through faith in the gospel, God gives us new life (2:5). According to 2 Corinthians 5:17, the moment we put our faith in Jesus and His death, burial, and resurrection, we became new creations. The term "new creation" explains that what was once spiritually lifeless has been made alive. Believers are not a new species, like a cat becoming a dog. Rather, believers are brought to spiritual life, like a dead animal being brought back to life! The initial step of God's will for every Christian involves this internal transformation—God breathing life into the heart of a new believer.

 The initial step of God's will for every Christian involves this internal transformation—God breathing life into the heart of a new believer.

However, salvation is only the beginning. Most biblical instruction focuses on what we call progressive sanctification. God's will for believers is an ongoing process of internal transformation that continues each day after salvation until reaching heaven. As disciples take steps in sanctification, they walk the road of discipleship. Progressive sanctification is, therefore, the path of wisdom for every Christian.

On the path of wisdom and sanctification, attempting to clean up external aspects without addressing internal desires is futile. James addresses this issue in James 4:1, asking, "What causes quarrels and what causes fights among you? Is it not this, that your passions are at war within you?" (ESV). Actions are an outflow or overflow of our passions, or desires. Consequently, progressive sanctification must involve changes in our internal affection. God's will is accomplished within us disciples as we transform to desire what Jesus desires, to love as Jesus loves, and to prioritize what Jesus prioritizes. If we desire to understand God's will, a disciple must grasp the concept of sanctification.

 God's will is accomplished within us disciples as we transform to desire what Jesus desires, to love as Jesus loves, and to prioritize what Jesus prioritizes.

Another significant passage that speaks directly to progressive sanctification is 1 Thessalonians 4:1–8. Verse 3 states, "For this is the will of God, your sanctification" (ESV). Sanctification pertains to personal holiness. Since God is holy, he desires believers to be holy as well. Verse 7 emphasizes our holiness: "God has not called us for impurity, but in holiness." Pursuing sanctification entails striving for purity and holiness. So, how do disciples live sanctified lives and become holy?

Progression Is Not Perfection

First, daily sanctification, or internal transformation, does not demand perfection. Sanctification occurs gradually, day by day, as we disciples take steps of confession and communion with God. External obedience naturally follows these daily steps, but a person should not allow an external measure to be the sole measurement of discipleship success.

Changing Affections

While disciples should never neglect external obedience, we should focus on addressing motives and desires. Changing our affections leads to lasting sanctification.

In fact, our personal virtue flows from our ongoing pursuit of truth and love. First Thessalonians 4:3–6, where Paul commands the Thessalonians to abstain from sexual immorality (4:3), describes this progression, or cultivation of character. God's will of sanctification includes specific sexual ethics for believers to exemplify, and these external ethics demand correct motives. God's holy standard of self-control and submission flows from within, described in verse 5: "not in passionate lust like the pagans, who do not know God." "Passionate lust" refers to strong desires that motivate external actions. Making sexually pure decisions without a genuine transformation of desire is like trying to assemble a puzzle from the outside. It does not produce lasting change on the inside.

Renewal of the Mind

Sanctification also progresses through the renewal of the mind. Romans 12:1–2 is another passage that instructs believers in progressive sanctification. Verse 2 emphasizes the importance of a believer's thought patterns: "Do not conform to the pattern of this world, but be transformed by the renewing of your mind. Then you will be able to test and approve what God's will is—his good, pleasing, and perfect will." Whereas the term "passion" in 1 Thessalonians 4:5 refers to a believer's affections and emotions, "your mind" in Romans 12:2 pertains to our thoughts concerning truth and falsehood.

The word "renewing" in Romans 12:2 is distinct to Christian literature and always highlights the work of the Holy Spirit within us believers. The Holy Spirit brings about internal change; then, through this renewal, we discern and prove God's will. Verse 2 describes God's will as good, perfect, and pleasing. Understanding what is good, perfect, and pleasing will help us make right choices. Discovering God's will directly results from the internal transformation brought about by the Holy Spirit, who does His work in the realm of the mind and heart.

> Discovering God's will directly results from the internal transformation brought about by the Holy Spirit, who does His work in the realm of the mind and heart.

These two passages, 1 Thessalonians 4 and Romans 12, caution believers against fixating solely on external matters and neglecting internal ones. Internal transformation does not magically solve all of life's puzzles, but it is God's method of guiding His children through the trials He sovereignly allows. Discipleship will always involve learning and obeying the commands of Scripture as the Holy Spirit and God's Word progressively transform our hearts and minds.

Question: What is God's will?

Answer: God's will is to transform me internally.

Bible Passages for Further Study

- Ephesians 2:1–10
- Titus 3:3–8
- 1 Thessalonians 4:1–8
- Romans 12:1–2
- Colossians 3:1–2

Personal Reflection

1. When have you wondered about "God's will"?

2. What usually prompts you to consider what God's will is for you?

3. Have you believed the gospel of Jesus Christ, beginning the work of internal transformation?

4. What loves, desires, and motives exist in you? Try making a list.

5. How can others pray for you as you seek God's will of internal transformation?

6. About what specific areas of spiritual need could you talk to a mentor or pastor?

How Does God Accomplish His Will?

Before we consider how God accomplishes His will, let's review what God's will is. God's will is to transform believers—to transform you—internally.

Trials: The Valley between Knowledge and Character

Internal transformation begins with salvation, progresses during earthly life, and culminates in heavenly glory. Progressive sanctification encompasses both internal and external obedience and results in fruit. Spiritual fruit grows as the internal roots of desires, motives, and loves transform. Successful discipleship, therefore, begins with the internal transformation of the heart, which leads to changes in external actions. In other words, outward fruit naturally follows the transformation of inner roots.

To accomplish internal transformation, God provides daily opportunities that foster spiritual growth. He gives unique spiritual training through tests and trials tailored to individual believers. God's desire to transform believers rests behind each test and trial you encounter.

Perhaps you are familiar with gospel tracts, those little booklets, pamphlets, or faux million-dollar bills that creatively illustrate the gospel message. One famous tract employs the metaphor of a bridge to depict the gospel message. This bridge illustration teaches the gospel and helps represent progressive sanctification as well.

Imagine a person standing on the edge of a vast gorge or canyon. One side symbolizes humans/sinfulness, and the other side, across the canyon, symbolizes God/heaven. No one can bridge the gap between sin and God. Jesus and His righteousness alone bridge this gap, providing the only path for sinners to reconcile with God. Most bridge-style tracts depict a cross lying horizontally over the chasm, illustrating Christ's death and resurrection as the means of human reconciliation, because the gospel repairs humanity's broken relationship with God the Father.

A similar bridge illustration applies to sanctification, with a few conceptual differences. A believer seeking internal transformation is comparable to the person in the bridge tract. A wide gap exists between the believer's human nature and Christlike, transformed character. Each Christian stands at a Grand Canyon–sized gulf, necessitating significant assistance to reach the other side. God provides this assistance through spiritual training and uses challenging tests and trials to bridge the gap in our sanctification.

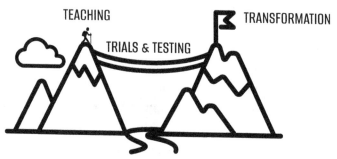

It is important to note that knowledge alone does not produce transformation. Many religious individuals possess extensive knowledge of God's Word but fail to experience actual change. Knowing the names and order of the books of the Bible, memorizing specific verses, or understanding theological views remains distinct from possessing genuine wisdom, or grasping the purpose and meaning of truth and applying that knowledge to daily life. *Wisdom lives out the truth by aligning what the person loves with what Jesus loves.* Mere knowledge of a sinful action does not automatically enable a disciple to follow Jesus's commands or avoid prohibited behavior. Wisdom begins with a fear or love of God, including loving what he loves. God allows tests and trials in a disciple's life to cultivate wisdom from knowledge.

Spiritual training (i.e., tests and trials) creates the path that moves us disciples from acquisition of knowledge about God's Word to transformation of our character. Every disciple must, therefore, learn and understand the Word of God. As we grasp the teachings of God's Word, God provides spiritual training to transition our rote knowledge into wisdom. Additionally, the path of spiritual training beckons us to walk with God through deep, dark, rugged valleys.

 As we grasp the teachings of God's Word, God provides spiritual training to transition our rote knowledge into wisdom.

Deuteronomy 8:1–6 and James 1:1–3 provide examples of how God facilitates internal transformation through tests and trials. These passages highlight how training serves as a bridge between teaching and transformation.

A Really Long Camping Trip

Deuteronomy 8 recounts Moses's speaking to the second generation of Israelites who came out of Egypt. The first generation, rebellious and lacking wisdom, failed to heed God's Word through Moses, which resulted in their death in the wilderness. One of

God's primary purposes for Israel's forty years of wilderness wandering was to allow the entire first generation to die. However, God had another purpose in the wilderness, specifically for the second generation of Israel.

Over forty years, God tested and humbled the second generation to reveal what was in their hearts—the real root of why they struggled to obey His commands (8:2). Their problem was not poor leadership or lack of provisions. Their problem was their failure to recognize the sinful state of their hearts. The *Shema* (a Jewish prayer) in Deuteronomy 6:4 instructed the people to love the Lord with all their hearts, yet people do not naturally possess love for God. God led Israel through the wilderness to produce this love through trials. Physical hunger, for example, exposed the Israelites' lack of trust, prompting them to turn to and believe in God and His faithful promises. Just as God led Israel through humbling tests in the wilderness, he continues to train disciples through difficult valleys. Trials still increase our trust and love for our heavenly Father.

> Moments of suffering provide opportunities for the knowledge of God's word to blossom into wisdom.

A quick comparison with James 1:1–3 supports this idea. James encouraged dispersed and suffering believers to rejoice amid trials, with the understanding that these tests would produce fruit. In short, God permits suffering and trials to bring about transformation. Moments of suffering provide opportunities for the knowledge of God's Word to blossom into wisdom. Thus, spiritual training links knowledge and character, leading disciples to transformation through tests and trials. Christlikeness forms at the humbling depths of a trial, not during the high points of life.

> Christlikeness forms at the humbling depths of a trial, not during the high points of life.

To recap, successful discipleship begins with understanding God's will of internal transformation. God facilitates this internal transformation by providing spiritual training through tests and trials. Recognition of trials then leads to further growth and development in discipleship. In the coming questions (chapters), we will examine why trials uniquely provide sanctifying opportunities.

Question: How does God accomplish His will?

Answer: God provides spiritual training in the form of tests and trials.

Bible Passages for Further Study

- Deuteronomy 8:1–6
- James 1:1–3
- 1 Peter 1:3–9
- 1 Peter 4:1–6

Discussion Questions

1. What activities or events do people normally seek when they want transformation?

2. What activities or events does God provide to produce transformation in believers?

3. What recent trials has God allowed in your life?

4. In what ways has God been training you?

5. How have trials helped you notice your heart's desires, motives, or loves?

How Do My Trials Cultivate Transformation?

Please review the questions and answers from the previous chapters: What is God's will for you? God's will for you is to transform you internally. How does God accomplish His will of internal transformation? God provides spiritual training in the form of tests and trials.

Now consider how your trials cultivate your transformation.

Trials: How God Reveals the Heart

Brad had struggled with pornography and masturbation for many years. What began as a few tempting pictures on social media developed into a full addiction, costing Brad time and money as a college student. Brad sought out his friend Greg to help him with his problem.

"How did this week go?" asked Greg.

"I was having a great week . . . until Friday night. Everything was fine, but then, out of nowhere, I started wanting to look at pornography. I gave in again and fell. What am I doing wrong?" answered Brad.

"Did you have any other struggles or trials throughout the week, Brad?" Greg asked.

"What do you mean?" questioned Brad.

"Well, desires in our heart don't just appear out of nowhere. Did you have any other trials this week, even something you thought was unrelated to your struggle with lust?"

After thinking briefly, Brad replied, "Well, actually, yeah. My disagreement with my boss on Monday night got out of control. That led to arguments with coworkers the next day. I was upset when I got home from work on Tuesday."

Greg gently asked, "What desire was at work within your heart during those conflicts with your boss and coworkers?"

"Anger, I guess. I didn't like how things were going at work and got angry with them. I felt like everything was out of my control. I was the only one working hard, but I'm the one that got in trouble with the boss! It was their fault, and they needed to know about it," Brad answered. Greg could tell Brad was still a bit upset about those circumstances.

Greg continued, "You stated that you were having a good week until Friday, but maybe God allowed the temptation to show you something in your heart from earlier in the week. Do you think your anger at work and your lust at home are related?"

"Yes, I think they are," Brad agreed, "and I don't know what to do. Can you help me learn from these trials?"

Trials: How God Cultivates Spiritual Awareness

God's will is to transform our hearts internally, including our loves, desires, and motives. This transformation happens through spiritual training, which comes through tests and trials. While God may not lead us through extended periods of testing as He did with the Israelites in the wilderness, He consistently provides difficulties as opportunities for spiritual growth. So, what makes difficulties, tests, and trials unique in cultivating spiritual transformation?

Preparing the Ground

Cultivation is a farming or gardening term that means "preparation and use for the raising of crops." Seeds planted on hard soil need help to grow correctly, if at all. Before they are planted, the field needs to be softened and tilled, or cultivated. The soil is turned over, dug up, and sifted. Seeds planted deep into cultivated soil yield more abundant fruit. Typically, before growth can occur, the soil requires stirring. Similarly, God uses trials to cultivate, or foster growth in, the soil of our hearts, allowing his Word to take root and flourish.

Trials function as cultivators in a believer's life. They disrupt and restrict our desires. Like a child who cries and throws a tantrum when denied a desired toy or candy, our hearts react when our loves and motives are restricted. God understands our desires, and He designs and employs trials to stir up the soil and reveal those desires. Through applying pressure, God brings growth.

Applying Pressure for Growth

Objects under pressure release what is inside. Consider a tube of toothpaste. When people purchase toothpaste, they believe the tube contains toothpaste, even though they can't see it at first. Verification comes when they squeeze the tube causing toothpaste to emerge. Gentle pressure applied to the tube reveals its contents, confirming toothpaste, we hope, and not some other substance!

We see the same principle with tea. What happens when a bag of tea, packed tightly with leaves and spices, is immersed in a mug of boiling water? The slow steeping process begins as the bag bobs up and down, and the hot water draws out the flavors, aroma, nutrients, and caffeine. The pressure and heat facilitate the extraction of what is on the inside.

Similarly, God uses tests and trials like pressure on a tube of toothpaste or the hot water that brews tea. These tests and trials reveal what is truly happening in our hearts. Let's recall Deuteronomy 8:2, which records how God used the difficulties in the wilderness to unveil what desire was at work in the Israelites' hearts. The Israelites desired various things—food, water, better leadership, safety, and more—and they were upset when their desires went unfulfilled. God consistently tested them in those areas, and each test exposed the actual contents of their hearts: complaint, bitterness, hate, and envy.

Becoming Aware of What's Inside

People mostly remain ignorant of what is happening inside their hearts. However, through the pressure of spiritual training, what is inside begins to surface. Our most straightforward response is to avoid the issues within, but *successful discipleship teaches us to pause and examine ourselves*. Discipleship involves becoming intentionally and spiritually aware of the heart. God cultivates this spiritual awareness to help us connect our external actions and speech to the internal realities. Just as a loving father disciplines his child, God disciplines us through trials, which serve as tools for Him to reveal what is truly in our hearts.

 Discipleship involves becoming intentionally and spiritually aware of the heart.

Take a moment to find five books, preferably of assorted sizes. Stack the books in the shape of a pyramid, with the largest on the bottom. Each book represents a category of concern in our spiritual lives. The top two books represent the external aspects: what we do and what we say. When a test or trial occurs, our actions and speech reveal our inner selves. As disciples, we learn to connect these two external categories with three categories on the inside.

The bottom three books represent the inner self: what we think, what we feel, and why we do what we do. God desires to transform the loves at the bottom, knowing that what starts in the heart progresses to the top.

We can react or respond swiftly when a trial or test cuts off our desires deep within (James 4). Our trials and their pressure reveal our thoughts, emotions, and motives; this awareness in turn helps us respond correctly during trials. If we can discern incorrect loves, motives, and desires, we can turn from them and repent. Because of this, we can consider trials a joy because they expose our internal issues.

Question: How do my trials cultivate transformation?

Answer: Trials increase awareness of what I love.

Bible Passages for Further Study

- Deuteronomy 8:2
- Proverbs 4:23
- Jeremiah 17:5–10
- Matthew 15:1–20

Discussion Questions

1. What events has God allowed in your life to "cultivate" your heart?

2. Can you identify how a trial revealed your inner thoughts, emotions, or desires? Describe what happened.

3. When God applies pressure on you, how do you normally respond?

4. Whom do you normally turn to for help during a trial?

What Forms of Training Is God Using in My Life?

Before you consider the forms of training God is using in your life, review the past questions and answers:

Q1: What is God's will?

Answer: God's will is to transform me internally.

Q2: How does God accomplish His will for my internal transformation?

Answer: God provides training in the form of tests and trials.

Q3: How do my trials cultivate transformation?

Answer: Trials increase awareness of what I love.

This chapter considers three kinds of trials we believers face during the process of transformation, and why we face them.

The Revelation of Internal Issues through External Trials

Ed had reached his limit with his wife's behavior and manner of speaking to him. He couldn't contain his frustration as he drove home from lunch with his friend Aaron.

"She just never listens and refuses to take any responsibility!" Ed exclaimed. "If only she would keep quiet and stop saying hurtful things, I wouldn't react and fight back. Why can't she see that?"

Aaron listened attentively, waiting for the right moment to interject. After a brief silence, he posed a question to Ed: "Do you genuinely believe your wife is the root issue causing these fights?"

Ed felt confused, thinking he might have misunderstood Aaron's question. "Of course she's the problem! Every argument starts because of her. I come home after a long day at work, and all she does is criticize and point out my flaws as a husband. She's the issue here."

Aaron paused for another moment, then repeated his question. He went on, "I understand that you feel she provokes the fights, but do you think she's truly responsible for causing them?"

This time, Ed caught the gentle tone in Aaron's voice, recognizing that his friend was trying to make a point he had missed. Aaron did this occasionally, always out of love and a desire to help Ed grow.

"Well, if she's not the real problem, what is?"

"I'm wondering," Aaron carefully suggested, "whether God is allowing these challenges with your marriage to reveal something about your own heart."

By this time, Ed had returned home and parked his truck in the garage. They sat silent for a moment or two until Aaron inquired if Ed had a Bible. They read James 4:1–10 together, going through the verses a few times.

"I guess God is using my wife to work on me, right?" Ed acknowledged.

Aaron smiled as he replied, "Yes, I suppose He is. Welcome to the club; God's doing the same thing in my life too!"

Trials play a crucial role in cultivating transformation by making us more aware of our loves, desires, and motives (as we learned in chapter 3). In His sovereignty, God permits various categories of trials. Our ability to identify these types of trials enhances our daily discipleship, because recognizing these categories is invaluable for progressive sanctification for ourselves and those we help. The three primary types of trials are difficult people, adverse circumstances, and temptation.

Trial #1: Difficult People

If you're anything like me, you've experienced anger or frustration with numerous people. James 4 addresses these moments of interpersonal conflict. James 4:1 asks, "What causes fights and quarrels among you?" Wars and fights typically involve other people, and James's recipients were no exception.

A frequent problem in human relationships is the existence of hidden expectations. We desire others to respect, love, and serve us. However, others often fail to meet our hidden expectations, and this failure produces difficulties. Perhaps there'd be less conflict if our friends and loved ones simply did what we expect. Since everyone falls short of human expectations, it's no surprise that people become a significant source of conflict. Further, many Christians struggle to understand God's purpose in allowing our interpersonal conflicts.

His purpose is for us to become aware of the desires that fuel our external conflict. These desires progress from the inside to the outside (Jas 4:1–2), with unmet expectations escalating into fleshly attitudes and sinful actions. James 4:2 states, "You desire and do not have, so you murder" (ESV). Murder is simply the aggressive manifestation of unmet desires within the heart. We can find examples of this murderous progression dating back to the beginning—Cain desired; Cain didn't receive; Cain murdered Abel (Gen 4:1–16).

While most individuals refrain from fulfilling their desires through murder, Jesus, in the Sermon on the Mount, sought to address the internal motivations behind murder:

You have heard that it was said to those of old, "You shall not murder; and whoever murders will be liable to judgment." But I say to you that everyone who is angry with his brother will be liable to judgment; whoever insults his brother will be liable to the council; and whoever says, "You fool!" will be liable to the hell of fire. (Matt 5:21–22 ESV)

God uses our conflicts with difficult people to reveal the anger and other fleshly desires within our hearts.

 God uses our conflicts with difficult people to reveal the anger and other fleshly desires within our hearts.

Trial #2: Adverse Circumstances

Trials often involve messy circumstances instead of difficult people. These moments or situations involve challenges, such as an overwhelming workload, frustrating vehicle repairs, awkward family developments, health crises, or monetary loss. Fill in the blank with whatever adverse circumstance God has allowed in your life—these are messy moments when God turns up the heat and applies pressure.

Most Christians experience messy circumstances but often neglect to see the significance of those circumstances to their personal spiritual journeys. In his first epistle, Peter reminds believers that joy and adversity mix and that trials are intentional for purifying the heart. He wrote, "In this you rejoice, though now for a little while, if necessary, you have been grieved by various trials, so that the tested genuineness of your faith—more precious than gold that perishes though it is tested by fire—may be found to result in praise and glory and honor at the revelation of Jesus Christ" (1 Pet 1:6–7 ESV).

While God yearns for transformed hearts, we yearn for comfort instead of adversity. While our fleshly nature reacts with resistance and conflict, God seeks to train us in humility and submission to His perfect plan. He refines us by restricting our desires during difficult circumstances.

Trial #3: Resistance to Temptation

Alongside difficult people and adverse circumstances, temptation to sin reveals our internal issues. We can either disobey God's commands, or we can resist temptation. We all experience temptation, but not all resist it. God allows us to be tempted as a test that reveals our hearts' desires. Resisting temptation reveals a heart and mind under the control of God's Spirit and Word.

It's important to remember that God does not directly tempt us believers when we face sinful urges. James 1:13–15 states,

Let no one say when he is tempted, 'I am being tempted by God,' for God cannot be tempted with evil, and he himself tempts no one. But each person is tempted when he is lured and enticed by his own desire. Then desire when it has conceived gives birth to sin, and sin when it is fully grown brings forth death." Though God allows sinful temptations under his sovereignty, James reminds believers that the root of temptation lies within the heart. Nevertheless, temptation serves as spiritual training for us to internally submit our desires to God's will.

> Though God allows sinful temptations under His sovereignty, James reminds believers that the root of temptation lies within the heart.

To recap, when we go through trials and diligently search for which type of trial we are encountering, we engage in God's will of transformation. God uses these trials to facilitate the work of progressive sanctification. Additionally, identifying these trials helps us recognize the precise moments when God is sanctifying and transforming us.

Question: What forms of training is God using in my life?

Answer: God uses three forms of training: difficult people, adverse circumstances, and temptation.

Bible Passages for Further Study

- James 1:1–3
- James 4:1–10
- 1 Peter 1:3–9
- Matthew 5:21–26

Discussion Questions

1. Are any of your relationships strained by conflict?

2. What circumstances stress you the most?

3. Can you articulate why they are stressful?

4. What difficult people, circumstances, or temptations do you remember from this past week?

5. What desires did God confront through the trials He allowed this past week?

6. What sins are you most tempted to give in to, and how well are you doing at resisting those temptations?

7. What desires, loves, and motives are connected to your temptations?

Have I Been Responding Correctly to God's Spiritual Training?

Review the questions and answers from chapters 1 to 5:

Q1: What is God's will?

　　Answer: God's will is to transform me internally.

Q2: How does God accomplish His will of internal transformation?

　　Answer: God provides training in the form of tests and trials.

Q3: How do my trials cultivate transformation?

　　Answer: Trials increase awareness of what I love.

Q4: What forms of training is God using in my life?

　　Answer: God is using three primary categories of tests and trials to facilitate personal sanctification: difficult people, adverse circumstances, and temptation.

The Walk of Faith

In the walk of faith, understanding the progression from internal motives and desires to external actions during tests and trials is crucial. When faced with challenges, the sinful flesh reacts by promoting and preserving sinful desires. Common reactions include fighting through or fleeing from conflict. All believers naturally respond in wicked ways, but God desires that tests and trials train a correct response of yielded submission to the Holy Spirit and His Word.

 All believers naturally respond in wicked ways, but God desires that tests and trials train a correct response of yielded submission to the Holy Spirit and His Word.

Scripture identifies the way we should respond, that is, to "walk in the Spirit" rather than "walk in the flesh." Further discussion on these two "walks" will be provided in section 2. But before we can fix our walk, we believers must increase our spiritual awareness. As we have seen, God wants to reveal the heart, and discipleship requires our diligence in examining our internal desires, loves, and motives. Each test God sends presents an opportunity for us to examine and respond. The first goal in conflict is to recognize the battle within our hearts; the second is to yield to the Holy Spirit instead of the flesh.

Recognizing that error always precedes any correction, section 1 has focused on the spiritual recognition of errors within the heart. Through trials, God prompts us to change direction when our hearts veer off course. Then, when we recognize and acknowledge the sinful desires of our hearts, repentance and humility follow. God skillfully uses trials to increase our recognition of errors. Just as people don't believe the gospel without first recognizing their sin, learning to walk in the Spirit also requires recognition.

To recap, the sanctification journey is like a long road trip. No one reaches the destination without difficulty. Discernment concerning fleshly thoughts, emotions, and motives is a long-term project that requires cultivation and nurturing. God reveals these spiritual matters through our trials, and this spiritual recognition sets us on the path of growth and wisdom. With God's guidance, we face the real heart of our issues: the issues of the heart.

Practical Steps for Responding Correctly

How should a believer learn or attempt to grow in recognition or spiritual awareness? Practical steps for internal change seem more complicated than typical steps for improvement. Spiritual growth eludes someone checking boxes on a list or scheduled tasks. Nevertheless, here are three practical practices that will aid recognition and awareness in the discipleship process.

Journaling

Journaling is a great way to increase your awareness. Since God uses trials, why not track yours? The process of journaling requires careful thought and consideration as you record the events and their ramifications. Writing is always a helpful exercise for the mind, so writing about your own difficult experiences will help you think through scenarios. Journaling won't guarantee that you think correctly about your circumstances, but it will help prepare you to consider how to apply the knowledge you have gained.

As you journal, you should make two lists: all your trials (difficult people, adverse circumstances, and temptations) and all the loves, desires, and motives that those trials reveal. These lists require diligence and reflection. Looking squarely at your sinful heart will not be fun. The lists you make will help you slow down and consider the right and wrong path, even if you do so retroactively. God wants you to think about your trials correctly, and writing the tests and desires together will help you gain the perspective of wisdom. As much as possible, use biblical terms to name or address the loves, desires, and motives within your heart; this will allow Scripture to inform your perspective of these moments.

 God wants you to think about your trials correctly, and writing the tests and desires together will help you gain the perspective of wisdom.

Searching for Unresolved or Unreconciled Conflict

As mentioned earlier, spiritual awareness often eludes us until our wrong motives and desires manifest in our physical actions and affect others. Searching for unresolved or unreconciled conflicts is, therefore, another practical step to facilitate spiritual growth. Look over your trials for unresolved disputes with a spouse, family member, coworker, or church member. If you recognize something unresolved, the next practical step is confessing sin to God and the person.

Prioritizing Scripture Reading and Prayer in Your Daily Life

Both searching for unresolved conflict and confessing sin when you identify it assume you have a consistent devotional life involving Scripture reading and prayer. When you identify actions, speech, thoughts, emotions, or desires contrary to truth, remember that "God resists the proud but gives grace to the humble" (Jas 4:6). Therefore, "humble yourselves, casting all your cares on him because he cares for you" (1 Pet 5:6–7). Believers regularly and repeatedly react incorrectly in the face of trials, but the promises in James 4:6 and 1 John 1:9 remind us to quickly turn to God, praise Him for His abundant grace, and confess our sins. Try to incorporate the Word of God into your prayers. As you seek God's help in your growth, ask Him to accomplish what He has already stated in His Word. Praying the Word of God ensures you align your prayers with His will for you.

Question: Have I been responding correctly to God's spiritual training?

Answer: Yes or no—you must answer personally.

Bible Passages for Further Study

- Colossians 3:1–17

- Deuteronomy 6:4–9
- Matthew 22:34–40

Discussion Questions

1. Have you been responding well? Take time to write your answer.

2. How will you journal your sanctification journey?

3. Why is it helpful to identify your responses to the trials God has allowed?

4. Who is a spiritual mentor with whom you can discuss your responses to trials?

5. What steps would you need to take before you could offer help or insight to another believer walking through trials?

SECTION 2

RESPOND

LEARNING TO LIVE LIFE IN THE SPIRIT

What Are My Trials Revealing about Me?

One of the best features of modern technology is notifications on phones. I use a calendar app, a to-do list app, email, text, etc., on my smartphone; and I have a weird fascination with clearing the little red numbers on my screen that alert me to updates. Smartphones without notifications would be less smart, and the notifications aid in organizing a workday. Notifications are powerful tools.

Clear the Notifications

Imagine receiving a minor ding or buzz on your phone each time God sanctified you. "Excuse me, just a reminder. God wants you to recognize what is at work in your heart right now!" Even though it's not as flashy, God does have a notification system for believers. It's called trials and testing. God desires that we believers recognize what influences are at work within our hearts. Therefore, the first five questions (section 1) examine God's will for disciples to increase spiritual awareness in moments of trial. This notification system works unless we ignore it.

 Believers who see the issues in their hearts will start to grow. Thus discipleship progresses as recognition leads to response.

Believers who see the issues in their hearts will start to grow. Thus discipleship progresses as recognition leads to response. God's "spiritual notifications" alert us to our problems and issues that need solving. We believers clear these spiritual notifications when we respond correctly. *Correct responses include yielding to the Holy Spirit and the Word of God, cultivating contrition and repentance.*

Trials Reveal Spiritual Ruts

As we believers strive to respond correctly in a trial, our spiritual recognition brings short- and long-term benefits. Trials help, first, in the exact moment of trial. When, for example, your coworker speaks disrespectfully to you and the flesh reacts angrily, recognizing your anger in the moment of conflict provides helpful insight. Thus, seeing the real issue at work in your heart helps you avoid reacting with more sin or external sin. Part of God's plan of sanctification includes recognition and response in those precise moments of test and trial.

A second helpful dimension of spiritual recognition comes when we "zoom out" from the specific moment of trial and see larger patterns of reaction. We often experience negative emotions, attitudes, and thoughts that persist over multiple weeks and months. Long-term relationships with family, friends, coworkers, employers, and fellow church members allow us to connect the dots from our hearts to our actions on a much larger scale. Trials reveal how our long-held emotions, attitudes, and thoughts have been borne out in our consistent reactions/responses.

> Trials reveal how our long-held emotions, attitudes, and thoughts have been borne out in our consistent reactions/responses.

Each time a trial presents itself, we can walk down the path of our flesh or turn and walk the path of the Holy Spirit and the Word of God. Sometimes, though, we're unaware of how far down a wrong path we have traveled. Long-term spiritual patterns—good or bad—develop similarly to ruts in a muddy road.

The specific route over a muddy path is undetermined the first time someone walks or drives it. This undetermined path easily leads to sloshing and sliding back and forth. But frequent and consistent travel on the path solidifies and firms the rut, making future travel progressively easier. All of us believers have sinful ruts formed from fleshly reactions over extended periods. Spiritual recognition shows us these ruts. And when we correctly respond amid trials, we create new, godly spiritual ruts.

To clarify, difficult trials humble us, softening the hardened ruts within the heart; therefore, each trial offers an opportunity for us to cultivate new spiritual responses. We can view difficult people, adverse circumstances, and temptations joyfully because they further our spiritual growth by softening our hearts. Looking for and identifying larger spiritual patterns helps us learn new paths. Cultivating correct patterns of spiritual responsiveness is a daily responsibility for each disciple.

 If you can identify any fleshly, well-traveled ruts in your life, you can begin responding correctly and forming new spiritual ruts.

Think about your circumstances and look for spiritual ruts. These patterns of response or reaction reveal much about your relationship with God, especially with the Holy Spirit. We all tend to minimize sin in moments of trial, and we avoid addressing the larger patterns we struggle with. If you can identify any fleshly, well-traveled ruts in your life, you can begin responding correctly and forming new spiritual ruts.

What does a correct response look like? If the old ruts of the flesh are leading you to disobedience, you must learn to turn from the natural path and begin forming a new pattern of response.

Ultimately, the correct response is to remain yielded to the Holy Spirit and controlled by Him rather than by the flesh. Scripture calls this response "walking in the Spirit" and "being filled by the Spirit." We will address each of these biblical ideas in the following few chapters. But for now, we will explore a few practical ways to form new spiritual ruts.

Practical Steps to Form New Spiritual Ruts

Find a Friend to Help

Have you ever had a vehicle stuck in muddy or snowy conditions? Thankfully, I have only experienced this a handful of times (although writing about it will likely doom me to a few more). A few years back, I was hunting with friends visiting from out of state. Considering the season, I knew ahead of time that nobody should drive on certain roads on the family farm. With a hasty rejection of common sense, I drove my white Chevy Impala down a muddy road that appeared fine, at least at the start. I thought I was saving time by parking a tad closer to our hunting spot, but I quickly sacrificed those saved seconds while we waited to be pulled out by my neighbor and his tractor. For me, the value of that moment was the foresight it gave me for all future hunts; I never drove my Impala down that road at the farm again. I also learned the value of a good friend who owns a tractor! Word to the wise regarding hunting—just walk a few extra steps.

When it comes to our sanctification, muddy encounters and driving down new roads cannot be avoided. Discipleship requires some "off-roading," or navigation away from comfortable, sinful, and fleshly ruts. In these muddy moments, we need a friend and mentor who helps pull us through those muddy situations by providing encouragement, advice, and direction. When my car got stuck, the tractor and chain were necessary to get us out. Similarly, when we disciples begin to turn from our fleshly desires to take steps of obedience, we will be significantly helped by good friends, family members, and fellow Christians. Older and wiser people, such as parents or pastors, will know how to tow us out of sticky situations.

> All of us will grapple and struggle to learn wisdom, and God intends the path of wisdom to include good friends.

All of us will grapple and struggle to learn wisdom, and God intends the path of wisdom to include good friends. In fact, our struggle during sanctification will increase if we avoid seeking help. Part of fulfilling Christ's commission in Matthew 28 involves believers teaching other believers to obey God's Word. When we allow a spouse, friend, or fellow church member to help us form new patterns, we are participating in the great discipleship commission.

Craft a Wise Plan

Compiling a spiritual journal (p. 60) is a great way to stimulate personal reflection on recent trials. Recording details about your trials should lead you to anticipate when and how your flesh will react. In that way, reviewing previous reactions prepares future responses. Not only should you be able to reflect on your journal entries, but anyone helping in your discipleship will also benefit from understanding the ebbs and flows of your recent spiritual life and hold you accountable for forming new patterns.

You may hesitate to write your struggles down or share them with others, and you are not the only person to hesitate. No one enjoys focusing on his or her flaws, especially those revealed in the heart's deep, dark, and sinful caverns. Remember, sanctification is not perfection. The goal is not to have a shorter list of trials or a shorter list of fleshly reactions. *The goal is to develop a pattern of responding correctly during each trial—to cultivate faithfulness in sanctification. Spiritual responsiveness to God's training increas-*

es proportionately with the diligence we commit to the pursuit. Humble submission, not perfection, transforms us.

 While the process of sanctification takes a lifetime, patterns of submission to the Holy Spirit grow slowly, like investments.

While the process of sanctification takes a lifetime, patterns of submission to the Holy Spirit grow slowly, like investments. I wish we could snap our fingers and wake up changed tomorrow morning. But such giant leaps of transformation are reserved for when we first believe (regeneration) and when we die (glorification in heaven). Progressive sanctification is a long-term project, so crafting a long-term strategy for pursuing Christlike transformation works better than any quick, emotional fixes. A slow, steady, and faithful plan adds up over time.

Every disciple's plan of faithfulness will look different from every other disciple's plan, but all plans should include a few common elements. As mentioned, a good spiritual friend can guide you much further than you could reach alone—especially in muddy moments of confession and heartache. Related to this is consistency in your local church. A disciple who regularly forsakes the assembling of the local church (praying together, studying God's Word together, singing together, etc.) struggles to grow. The inverse is also true: a faithful church member typically bears more fruit. One last practical tip: a good sanctification plan should also include a forecast of what the disciple plans to digest, and I'm not talking potlucks! Carefully plan and consider both your sources of entertainment and your sources of spiritual nourishment.

Allow the Holy Spirit to Use the Word of God

Practical steps related to the Holy Spirit are challenging to discuss. Good, hearty trinitarian theology reminds us that the Holy Spirit possesses personhood and divinity precisely as the Father and the Son do. As a result, disciples need to develop the same reverence and dependence upon the Holy Spirit as on our Savior and heavenly Father.

The problem comes when we understand dependence on the Holy Spirit as some mystical or magical experience. Dependence on the Holy Spirit comes through prayerful application of God's Word, and obedience to the Word remains the minimum test of a believer's submission to the Holy Spirit.

In answering question 2 (pp. 37-42), we discussed the bridge illustration as a tool for considering the process of sanctification. We saw that transformation follows training, which follows teaching. Spiritual training occurs in moments of trial when the *teaching of God's Word* applies directly to us. God's Word helps bring recognition in our hearts and in our taking active steps of obedience. Disciples seeking wisdom never find it without the Word of God.

The Spirit works through the Word of God (John 17:17), which is the sword of the Spirit. Consequently, walking in the Spirit must involve His Word. Nothing is more practical than incorporating the Word of God directly into moments of trial. Where do you run for support, truth, or comfort in your difficult moments? Most people distract themselves from difficulties by using people, music, games, phones, social media, friends, and the like. These things are not necessarily bad, but our main goal during a trial should not be to feel better or avoid our heart issues. We should seek the Holy Spirit's work within us, and one of the best ways to allow this process is to incorporate God's Word into moments of difficulty.

 We should seek the Holy Spirit's work within us, and one of the best ways to allow this process is to incorporate God's Word into moments of difficulty.

Do you allow God's Word to be present in suffering, or do you seek other sources of strength or help? Patterns of response to the Word will follow our spiritual ruts, so applying the Word in moments of reaction will help us form new spiritual ruts. Memorizing verses will help set our minds at critical moments. So, choose several verses and develop a pattern of submission during difficulty. Find ways to be mindful of truth in each trial.

Cease, Pray, Repent

Most of the time, believers simply need to pray more. We often react quickly, so try to *cease* impulsive action and *pray* instead. In those prayers, seek to identify and turn from any fleshly desires at work; *repent* of anything not under the control of the Holy Spirit. *Cease, pray, repent* (CPR) should provide a simple reminder to form new ruts.

My first pastor often reminded me "to pray the Word of God, so you know you're praying the will of God." Praying ideas and directives from Scripture intended for disciples guarantees that we are praying God's will (including sanctification through trials). Simple, scriptural prayers humble and transform us, inviting the Holy Spirit's direct access to our minds and hearts.

> Simple, scriptural prayers humble and transform us, inviting the Holy Spirit's direct access to our minds and hearts.

Considering these practical steps, make a game plan. Choose a verse or passage to memorize for the next time you encounter a trial. Think of creative ways to remind yourself to pray throughout the day or during a spiritual test. Imagine submitting to the Spirit on one of your typical days at school, work, home, and so forth; what does obedience look like? Consider developing patterns of walking in the Spirit through the Word in your difficulties.

Question: What are my trials revealing about me?

Answer: Trials reveal my patterns of spiritual response.

Bible Passages for Further Study

- Galatians 5:16–26
- John 15

Discussion Questions

1. How do most people respond to spiritual conflict?

2. What common distractions do people utilize to escape from recognizing internal conflicts?

3. Why is it difficult to get out of spiritual ruts on our own without help?

4. Have you developed any spiritual ruts, positive or negative?

5. Which friend or mentor will help pull you out of spiritual ruts?

6. What friendships do you currently have that do not help your spiritual journey?

7. What Bible verses would be most helpful during a trial?

Question 7

What Is Walking in the Spirit?

Before we consider the nature of walking in the Spirit, let's review question and answer 6: What are my trials revealing about me? Trials reveal my patterns of spiritual response.

Living Life with the Spirit

Once spiritual recognition takes place, disciples learn to respond to God's notifications (trials and tests). We are responsible each day for responding to trials with submission to the Holy Spirit. The New Testament describes the correct response as "walking in the Spirit" and "being filled with the Spirit." These are opposite sides of the same coin. We disciples must learn to allow the Holy Spirit to control us (our walk in the Spirit), and the Holy Spirit will produce His fruit in the heart (His filling us). Authentic Spirit control is the essence of discipleship—genuine character transformation produced by the Holy Spirit.

 Authentic Spirit control is the essence of discipleship—genuine character transformation produced by the Holy Spirit.

When a sinner is born again, that person becomes indwelled by the Holy Spirit. Just as the Holy Spirit dwelled in the tabernacle and temple in Old Testament times, the Holy Spirit now resides within each of us believers (1 Cor 6). He shares the same divine essence as the Father and the Son, so God himself dwells within each of us. His indwelling presence should affect our whole pattern of life.

Galatians 5:16–26 commands each believer to "walk in the Spirit," so a disciple seeking to obey God's Word must learn to yield control to the work of the Holy Spirit. This passage describes the Holy Spirit's control in numerous ways. Believers are to be "led by the Spirit" and must continue "being in step with the Spirit." Adversely, gratifying the desires of the flesh, living "under the law," or producing fleshly fruit (5:19–20) depicts the opposite of walking in the Spirit. Possessing both a fleshly nature and the Holy Spirit, we believers must learn how each one influences our internal and external lives.

Walking in the Spirit Is a War

Galatians 5 describes a spiritual fight for control. The sinful flesh—and its loves, motives, and desires—*will fight for control* with the Holy Spirit and the conscience within our hearts. In this war, a controlled response or passionate reaction determines obedience or failure to obey God's commands. As disciples we walk in the Spirit by allowing the Holy Spirit, rather than the flesh, to control our hearts and actions.

Unsurprisingly, these opposing powers have drastically different outcomes. Therefore, whoever wins the battle gains control and affects our internal and external fruit. The genuine fruit of Christian virtue and character flows from walking under the Spirit's control, and all the opposite fleshly fruits result from obeying sinful lusts and passions. The fruits are the prize of the winning fighter, who thus wins control. Therefore, the key to spiritual growth is for us to yield to the Spirit so he wins and defeats the flesh.

Walking in the Spirit Is *NOT* an Emotion

Walking in the Spirit does not require perfection or perfect affection. We often become discouraged due to meager or weak devotion to God. We assume that the mere presence of opposing loves constitutes failure. Galatians, however, teaches the opposite: believers should plan on the internal conflict of competing desires. The whole picture is a fight, and it takes two to tango.

The tension of Spirit and flesh in the heart involves fierce emotion and attitudes. To yield to the Holy Spirit instead of the flesh *almost always* consists in choosing contrary to strong desires, loves, and motives. Jesus knew this when he asked His disciples to "deny" themselves, take up their cross, and follow Him. Discipleship necessitates a choice against personal desire. If we choose fleshly desire, we decide against the desires of the Spirit. If we choose right, we decide against the desires of the flesh. Most of the time, making this choice will not *feel* great.

 Discipleship requires yielding to the Spirit regardless of emotion.

Walking in the Spirit is not a particular emotion or feeling. A choice to yield control to the Holy Spirit actually brings emotions and motives into tension. Waiting to *feel* motivated or perfect about obedience to the Holy Spirit is a fool's game; perfect affections may never come. Discipleship requires yielding to the Spirit regardless of emotion. Consequently, *spiritual training involves obedience contrary to emotions*.

Be aware, however, that choosing obedience contrary to emotions does not mean we ignore opposing emotions within our hearts when they become evident. After all, God leads us through trials specifically to reveal this inner war of Spirit and flesh. We should never ignore incorrect affections and motivations but should, rather, train ourselves to respond appropriately.

We should never ignore incorrect affections and motivations but should, rather, train ourselves to respond appropriately.

To recap, cultivating specific and ordinate, or aligned, affections will take time and sacrifice. Discipleship requires us to make decisions with mixed spiritual desires. While our emotions are real, they are not always true. Therefore, emotions should not drive our commitment to the Lord and His ways.

Walking in the Spirit Is, at a Minimum, Obedience to God's Word

Although walking in the Spirit is not a feeling, it also cannot be anything *less than* obedience to the commands of God's Word. Simply put, a disciple walking under the Spirit's control does not indulge fleshly desires. Spirit control always leads a believer to obey what God has asked. However, I know from my experience—and maybe you do too—that I can do the right actions for the wrong reasons. I'm often quite aware of my impure motives. The fact is, we can *perform* the external motions of obedience to God's Word without being controlled by the Holy Spirit.

Thus, obedience to God's Word is not purely an external action. Every decision to obey involves the heart's loves, desires, and motives. Thankfully, God discerns and judges the heart, and it is not up to any individual to judge another's motives. When we as individual disciples seek to obey God's Word, we must personally address the internal motivations behind our decisions.

An example from James is impure prayer. All believers know they should pray. James addressed praying people, but they prayed so they might "spend it on [their] pleasures." This kind of prayer constitutes a correct action with an incorrect motive. James 4, therefore, reminds us that walking in the Spirit is not *only* external obedience to God's Word but is also internal correction of our heart motives.

We cannot wholly escape the presence of the flesh, but our goal in walking in the Spirit is the continual growth of Christ-honoring loves, desires, and motives. Wanting the fleshly desires of our hearts to magically disappear would be unrealistic and unwise. *The presence of the flesh serves as a daily reminder of our immense spiritual need for character transformation*. Therefore, do not become discouraged over the competing presence of the flesh, but also do not allow yourself to become complacent to the point of ignoring your flesh's influence on your heart. Genuine recognition *and* response to the presence of our flesh is the essence of walking in the Spirit. *Walking in the Spirit is, therefore, choosing to yield control to the Holy Spirit amid competing, fleshly desires*. It is a choice to seek the enabling grace of God for us to keep His Word and to walk in His ways. Walking in the Spirit involves the deepest loves and heart motives, just as it involves outwardly keeping Christ's commands. Simply put, walking in the Spirit makes the right choices fueled by the right loves.

> It is a choice to seek the enabling grace of God for us to keep His Word and to walk in His ways.

Practical Steps to "Keep Up" with the Holy Spirit

Look again at the lists of fruits in Galatians 5. The first list is fruits associated with the control of the flesh, and the second is the fruits of the Spirit. Notice how many of these fruits have an internal component that reflects externally. For example, the first fruit of the Holy Spirit listed is *love*. Does that mean, that I *desire* to love someone or that I choose to *act* lovingly?

The answer is both! The freedom of God's Spirit within allows us to choose the right action for the right reason. So, what should we believers do when we notice a lack of genuine love? When we, for instance, desire to wrong others, think evil thoughts toward a brother or sister, or yearn to lash out in anger, we should apply CPR: cease, pray, and repent. Turning away from the sinful desires within (repentance) and seeking comfort and strength in the Word of God are the steps in the walk of the Spirit. We confess our sin and commune with the Spirit.

Often recognition of a fleshly walk comes after sin has spilled out of the heart. When this is the case, walking in the Spirit involves reconciliation, which begins by our seeking God's cleansing and asking Him to forgive our fleshly actions. Reconciliation also requires going to the person(s) we have wronged, admitting that we were wrong, and asking that person(s) to forgive us. Genuine reconciliation humbles us, which is God's plan. God resists the proud but gives grace to the humble! A lack of repentant humility, on the other hand, stops our walk in the Spirit.

Can you identify patterns of the Spirit or flesh in you? Rather than looking at specific *moments,* look for larger spiritual patterns. Do you have patterns of the Spirit in your friendships, workplace, or home?

Question: What is walking in the Spirit?

Answer: Walking in the Spirit is living in obedience to God's Word under the Spirit's control.

Bible Passages for Further Study
- Galatians 5:16–26
- Romans 6:11–16
- Romans 8:1–17

Discussion Questions

1. What aspects of the fruit of the Holy Spirit do you struggle with, and which fruits do you do well with?

2. What results of the flesh, listed in Gal 5:19–21, do you struggle with?

3. What entries on the list of the flesh best describe some of your spiritual ruts?

4. Do you have moments planned in your day "to present yourself to God to be a slave of righteousness"?

5. When was the last conversation you had with someone else about your sin? Do you need more help?

What Is Being Filled with the Spirit?

Let's review the previous questions and answers in this section, "Respond—Learning to Live in the Spirit." What are my trials revealing about me? My trials reveal my patterns of spiritual response. What is walking in the Spirit? It is living in obedience to God's Word under the Spirit's control.

> What is walking in the Spirit? It is living in obedience to God's Word under the Spirit's control.

We have seen that discipleship involves the believer's correct response during difficulty. Trials increase spiritual recognition of the inner war between the Holy Spirit and the flesh, while discipleship encourages believers to learn to respond correctly. Then chapter 7 describes the correct response as "walking in the Spirit." This chapter discusses the other side of the same coin, "being filled by the Spirit." When believers "walk in the Spirit," they will also be "filled by the Spirit."

The Holy Spirit *Fills* When Believers *Walk*

We believers obey the command to walk in the Spirit when we recognize the work of the flesh, turn away from its desires, and yield control to the Holy Spirit. When the Holy Spirit is in control, He fills us with fruit from Him. Ephesians 5 describes filling in terms of control by contrasting the filling of the Spirit with being drunk with wine. Rather than being controlled or filled by alcohol, we can be filled by the Holy Spirit, who creates spiritual fruit within our hearts when we allow Him control. Further, when He is in control, He transforms us. Christlike fruit begins internally and extends to external obedience to God's Word. Progressive sanctification, therefore, depends on the filling that only the Holy Spirit produces. Our walking in and being filled with the Spirit are essential to our discipleship.

Galatians 5 presents two lists of fruit from different sources. Entries on both lists demonstrate that external virtues or vices overflow from internal character. Take love, the first entry on the list of Spirit fruit, for example. The term love refers to an affection or desire for another person, and loving actions often accompany internal affection. Additionally, both the flesh and the Holy Spirit have external avenues for expressions of love. The list of fleshly vices includes a handful of sexually deviant actions that manifest improper affections originating in the heart. In contrast, the Holy Spirit and His work within the believer enable a genuine response of love that includes proper internal desire (transformation) and proper external action (obedience). If we seek to display the fruit of love genuinely, we must first submit to and walk in the Spirit so that the Spirit fills us with love. These steps remain for all the spiritual virtues; the fruits of the Holy Spirit result from correct responses to our trials.

Though the presence and growth of spiritual fruit provides evidence that we are walking in and being filled by the Holy Spirit, we will never be perfect, at least in this life. Just as physical fruit takes time to grow, so spiritual fruit grows and blossoms over seasons of trial and testing. A consistent spiritual progression demonstrates transformation by the Holy Spirit. God desires to grow this fruit in each of us.

Consider Ephesians 5:18 and the command to be filled with the Holy Spirit in light of Galatians 5. Filling happens to us passively, meaning that we allow the Holy Spirit to fill us with the fruit. Galatians 5 describes these fruits as love, joy, peace, and so forth, although Ephesians 5 includes more expressions and demonstrations of the Spirit's fruit. The Spirit-filled believer in Ephesians 5 speaks and sings truth to others, overflows with thankfulness, and willingly submits to others. Thus, we believers learn to submit to and receive the ministry of the Holy Spirit within our hearts.

Walking through Seasons of Spiritual Growth

My father was a farmer. Some of my most precious memories come from my time on our farm in southeast Iowa. I often compare Iowa to the Shire in J.R.R. Tolkien's *The Lord of the Rings*. People here are good at growing stuff, much like the hobbits of the Shire. Sure, Iowans must adventure out to see mountains, but midwestern fields of corn and beans provide a suitable residence for all hobbit-like folks.

Although farming demonstrates how growing fruit requires work and time, it is also a reminder that growth does not rely entirely on the farmer. Here's an example: One season when I was a child, we harvested melons from the farm garden. One of my fondest childhood memories is eating those melons on the pickup's tailgate while watching the sun and my fishing bobber go down. Moments like that one made the harvest special. Everybody loves when the work is done and the fruit is ready!

But fruit comes at a cost. Fruit requires much time, effort, and growth. I remember planting those melons, watering the garden, and pulling and hoeing weeds in the scorching summer sun. Many days, believing my eyes, I thought nothing was happening. Day after day, the garden appeared the same, but at harvest when I saw the fruit, that harvest proved that growth had been taking place the whole time. Big watermelons don't pop up overnight; they grow over months of cultivation and nurturing.

Slow and steady growth happens spiritually too. As believers learn to walk in the Spirit, hearts and affections are transformed. Like me with the melons in the garden, a disciple might not see significant changes day by day. Often Christians look back months and years later, realizing that love, joy, peace, patience, and self-control blossomed as the perpetual and ongoing results of the Holy Spirit's increasing influence. To recap, trials lead us believers to yield more and more to the Spirit and the Word, and the Spirit, in turn, continues to transform us.

 Often Christians look back months and years later, realizing that love, joy, peace, patience, and self-control blossomed as the perpetual and ongoing results of the Holy Spirit's increasing influence.

Farming also reminds us who it is that truly controls growth. Yes, completing specific agricultural tasks increases the probability of fruit, but those tasks are not the fruit. Planting, pulling weeds, improving soil quality, watering, etc., all help the process; but none of those activities should be called fruit. The farmer cultivates the correct environment for growth, but the farmer alone cannot cause growth.

That is the way it is with spiritual progression too: "God gives the increase." The Holy Spirit transforms us as we read and meditate on God's Word, turn from sin, and cultivate proper affections in our hearts. The Holy Spirit causes our growth through Spirit filling. Therefore, living under the Holy Spirit's control is how we grow, are transformed, and produce fruit.

Since the Holy Spirit is not physically visible, without fruit as evidence someone might not even know the Spirit is present. The truth of this mystery should lead each of us deeper into worship and awe of the Creator, who lovingly and graciously dwells with us through His Spirit.

Practical Steps for Holy Spirit Filling

Being filled by the Holy Spirit and walking in the Spirit may feel mysterious; consequently, we must consider how Spirit filling, or control, works. Taking practical and visible steps helps us in the pursuit of transformation, even though external markers do not determine success.

Setting Goals

Setting goals is one of the steps in the pursuit of transformation, but spiritual goals are more difficult to craft than others. For example, a specific fitness goal may include reaching a certain weight or number. That is, specific fitness goals have clear targets, while spiritual goals may be unclear and imprecise. How then would someone track character development?

God's Word should be at least a minimum measurement in setting goals. For example, if you find yourself committing murder in your heart, you have a definitive marker, God's Word, that helps you know change is necessary. Your spiritual goals should align with Scripture.

Responding to Failure with Obedience

Another step is to responding to failure with obedience. Even as growth is taking place, we will give in to the flesh; and this failure may quickly discourage us in our spiritual progress. Strong feelings of guilt and shame may invade our minds and hearts. Although we should strive never to willfully give in to sin, faithful followers of Jesus are identified by a biblical response to failure. Sin will happen. Plan to never wallow in discouragement but to quickly pursue spiritual purity and reconciliation.

 Although we should strive never to willfully give in to sin, faithful followers of Jesus are identified by a biblical response to failure. Sin will happen. Plan to never wallow in discouragement but to quickly pursue spiritual purity and reconciliation.

Pursuing Self-Denial

One last practical step is to pursue self-denial, that is, restraining or limiting our own desires. Perhaps no other virtue proves more helpful to the journey of discipleship. Jesus himself qualified discipleship as a task requiring the denial of personal desires, but denial also involves choosing between competing desires. When someone determines to make spiritual changes by adding helpful activities, such as reading or praying more often, the flesh promotes alternatives. Read or sleep in? Go to church or work late? Numerous examples exist, as you know from personal experience. Eliminate the wrong desire by considering yourself "dead to sin and alive to God" because "you cannot serve two masters." So, deny yourself and turn away from the competition.

Question: What is being filled by the Spirit?

Answer: Allowing the Holy Spirit to produce growth.

Bible Passages for Further Study

- Ephesians 5:15–21
- Luke 8:1–18
- James 1:19–21

Discussion Questions

1.   In what ways have you seen the Holy Spirit fill you with His character and fruit?

2.   As you reflect on the fruits of the Spirit, what are specific areas of needed growth?

3.   When do you find yourself most out of control?

4.   What activities can you pursue, like a farmer, to allow the Spirit to cause growth?

5.   How might you help other people prepare for their own spiritual growth?

What Should I Do When I'm Not Walking in the Spirit?

So far in this section, we have asked, "What are my trials revealing about me?" and answered, "Trials reveal my patterns of spiritual response." We have also defined walking in the Spirit, which is living in obedience to God's Word under the Spirit's control. And we have asked, what is being filled by the Spirit? Being filled with the Spirit, we saw, is allowing the Holy Spirit to produce growth.

Considering the Correct Response

We have seen that God's will of internal transformation, or sanctification, takes place through spiritual training. Specifically, it involves walking in the Spirit and being filled by the Spirit rather than yielding control to the flesh. When believers yield control to the Holy Spirit, spiritual fruit is produced, and all facets of the Christian life grow and change under His control. One outcome of that growth and change is that we turn from a fleshly response to a godly response to sin.

The Bible uses many terms to describe a godly response to sin. This chapter focuses on four of them: yielding, humbling, submitting, and repenting. The path of discipleship includes learning and developing these virtuous, wise responses.

When God reveals the sinful heart at work, what do we believers do to continue walking in the Spirit and being filled with the Holy Spirit? If we respond correctly, we confess our sin and renew our communion with God. This recognition of and turning away from sin always precedes returning to Holy Spirit control. We believers are responsible to turn from sin and to walk in the Spirit. Then the Spirit fills us with spiritual fruit. Confession and communion are, therefore, two steps for us to take when we recognize we are being controlled by the flesh.

Yielding: Slow Down

The first word that helps describe a correct response is *yielding*. I first learned about yield signs when I learned to drive. I experience a "left turn yield" during each drive to my local coffee shop, where I love to work and am writing this. Yielding does not necessarily mean coming to a complete stop, but to yield, a driver must be aware of his car in relation to others in the intersection. Yielding, while driving, means to recognize that another car has the right-of-way; it means recognizing that the other driver is in control. Failure to slow down and assess your surroundings, failure to yield, could cause a collision with other cars in the intersection. Some-times, yielding does mean stopping and waiting for other drivers to work through the intersection first, and I need to yield even if I haven't yet had my morning coffee! Similarly, yielding to the Holy Spirit includes slowing down and honoring control.

At a busy intersection, a driver's failure to yield will likely lead to significant problems. Likewise, when we believers face difficulty and the flesh seeks control, we are in danger. We must consider who has the right-of-way at each spiritual intersection. Three pas-sages remind us of this principle: Colossians 3, 1 Thessalonians 5, and Ephesians 5.

Colossians 3:15 mentions letting the peace of God rule in our hearts. Peace is a fruit of the Holy Spirit, produced when the Holy Spirit leads and controls believers. The idea here is that peace would be the decision maker or the arbiter. Arbitration is a decision-making process, with the arbiter making the final call. To allow the peace of God to *arbitrate* within us, we must first allow the Holy Spirit to be in control. Therefore, we *yield* in moments of conflict, and the Spirit arbitrates instead of our flesh.

> To allow the peace of God to *arbitrate* within us, we must first allow the Holy Spirit to be in control. Therefore, we *yield* in moments of conflict, and the Spirit arbitrates instead of our flesh.

Next, 1 Thessalonians 5:19 mentions *not quenching* the Holy Spirit. The word here could also be translated *suppress* or *extinguish*. The command is to avoid suppressing or extinguishing the Holy Spirit. This command is the opposite side of the same coin from Colossians 3:15—we allow the Spirit to arbitrate; we do not suppress the Holy Spirit's control.

The Holy Spirit indwells each believer, but we often live as if He is absent. When we walk in the flesh, it hurts God. When we live in the flesh, we set the Holy Spirit aside. Think back to the busy intersection. What would happen if you disregarded the car that should be in control (the one with right-of-way)? If you choose not to yield, others might get hurt too.

The last passage to consider, Ephesians 5:18–19, does not mean that the Holy Spirit is an object poured into us, like water into a cup. Spiritual fruit fills us as the Holy Spirit produces it. He pours, or creates, the love, joy, peace, and other fruits. If the Holy Spirit is not in control because we have yielded to the flesh, Holy Spirit fruit is not produced. Consequently, as disciples we consistently demonstrate the filling of the master to whom we yield control.

How do we yield to the Holy Spirit? As I approach a busy intersection, I need to think about the laws of the road; following those commands is a great start. I must also apply driving instructions and maintain proper control of my vehicle! Spiritually, we do the same: follow the instructions in the Word of God. If you sense the flesh resisting God's Word, take time to pray, yielding yourself under the Holy Spirit's control through His warnings in God's Word.

> If you sense the flesh resisting God's Word, take time to pray, yielding yourself under the Holy Spirit's control through His warnings in God's Word.

Humbling: "Low" Down

The second word that helps describe a correct response is *humility*, or *humbling*. *Humbling* simply means "bringing low." The most challenging task God gives us each day is to humble ourselves, but the virtue of humility easily eludes us Christians in daily living. The flesh at work in our hearts despises genuine humility. In other words, our pride is one of the main aspects of the flesh. We often, and quite naturally, express little concern for the needs or desires of others.

In Deuteronomy 8, Moses reminds the Israelites of God's intentional affliction (humbling) of them in the wilderness. Humbling them was God's primary means of facilitating personal humbling. God afflicted to teach trust and worship. The trials God used for Israel seem so simple as I read them. I am fascinated that I experience the same ones! Are you easily agitated when you get hungry? God allowed Israel to be hungry, which facilitated personal humbling and the fear of the Lord. God designed a trial by hunger to increase the Israelites' spiritual awareness. First, he fed them in a strange way, unlike anything they had encountered previously. Next, he instructed them to gather the manna they needed daily, except before the Sabbath when they could gather twice the amount. No full pantry or leftovers for Israel! Thus, each family learned to trust God daily. This wilderness meal plan tested the Israelites' minds and hearts by reminding them of their true source and sustenance. They needed to recognize that God alone deserves worship; they needed humility to worship God instead of themselves. The same heart that struggled to gather only one day's worth of food would cause problems for obeying the rest of the law. God afflicted Israel to show the people that specific heart issue.

> They needed to recognize that God alone deserves worship; they needed humility to worship God instead of themselves.

Similarly, James 4 also ties humility with our proper response to the flesh, pointing out how our lack of humility separates us from God. Fleshly, worldly desires create conflict between us and the indwelling Spirit. Knowing the need for confession and communion, James reminded his readers that God extends grace only to the humble: "God resists the proud but gives grace to the humble."

While humility dictates much in our relationship with God, it also remains necessary as we interact with other people. Fleshly, prideful living will lead to sin against the people we live with. I don't know about you, but admitting my sin to others is often challenging. Why is it so difficult to admit fault? The flesh loves pride and hates humility.

We usually recognize the need to be humble, but admitting wrong and asking for forgiveness repulses us. Do you feel tension when you know you need to confess sin to someone and ask for that person's forgiveness? That tension demonstrates the influence of the flesh. The tension is the flesh's resistance against turning from its loves, desires, and motives.

Many times, when the flesh is at work, we become aware of what the morally right action and morally wrong action would be. For example, I rarely sin in complete ignorance; rather, I choose wrong with full knowledge. These moments display an intellect and heart in discord: I decide to act contrary to what I know to be true, allowing fleshly passions and affections to have control. Fleshly desire always promotes itself above the Lord and His Word. Therefore, the flesh needs to be brought low, humbled beneath the controlling presence of the Holy Spirit.

Submitting: Lay Down

The third word that helps describe our response is *submitting*. You may have noticed that submission has become less and less popular in society. It seems as if younger generations have a stronger sense of entitlement and struggle even more now to submit to authority than past generations did. My observation here is purely anecdotal, but it represents a common issue in our shared Christian experience. We all struggle to submit and lay down our rights.

When you think of submission, what comes to your mind? What does genuine submission look like for a believer? It looks like obedience to the Word of God. Submission should always conclude with external obedience, but it begins with the submission of our minds, hearts, desires, etc. We discussed this early in section 1, but the connection between loves, desires, and motives and our subsequent actions is essential. Our goal should be to turn from incorrect actions and attitudes. Genuine submission includes an internal component.

Repenting: Turn Around

The fourth and last word to describe a correct response is *repenting*. Repentance is turning or changing our minds about something. In the book of Acts, when sinners wanted to believe in Jesus Christ, Peter told them to repent, to turn from their sin to God. Repentance is likewise necessary in our progressive sanctification: internal submission recognizes the deviance of thoughts, emotions, and desires and turns from them.

One day, while a pastor, I received a phone call that pictures repentance quite well. For simplicity, I will refer to the caller with the generic "he." That church member was calling me from his car after a discipleship meeting took a confrontational turn. Events like that one provide great discipleship opportunities, because conflict never disrupts God's will of sanctification.

My call with the offended disciple was quite edgy. Anger, bitterness, and resentment are not as easy to discern over the phone, but I understood that the caller was upset. His tone oozed anger, as did his choice of words. Angry people enjoy accentuating a point by using worldly terminology, often including curse words. This caller's tone and words marked his frustration.

I responded by asking questions. Careful, well-crafted questions can significantly help a believer discern the work of the flesh in contrast to the Holy Spirit; for example, "Would the Holy Spirit produce that speech?" Another effective tactic is to quote Scripture: "Where do wars and fights come from?" A few such questions helped the caller recognize God's work of sanctification. Though he *recognized* his need for change, he also needed to respond correctly.

The beauty of that phone call was how it pictured both the internal and external acts of repentance. As the caller turned internally, he stopped driving in one direction and turned around. On that day, this believer recognized that he was heading in the wrong direction spiritually and geographically. He got off the highway at the next exit and turned his car around. The caller physically and spiritually *repented*.

Repentance often looks and feels like driving: we must turn away from sinful motivations and sinful disobedience while trials test our faithfulness to head in the right direction. Successful days of sanctification, at least for me, include several moments of turning and moving in the other direction. Although many believers consider perfection, or days without struggle, to be more indicative of sanctification success, they are deceived. Repentance, not cruising, offers the opportunity for genuine transformation. We grow through the trials that provide occasions for us to turn and drive in the other direction.

Patterns of Correct Response

All four words (*yielding, humbling, submission*, and *repenting*) should describe our response to God when we walk through trials. God intentionally makes "the drive" challenging so we will grow and be transformed! Each day brings opportunities for us to turn from the wrong way and drive in the other direction.

Consider the most recent trials you have experienced. How have you been responding to these difficulties? If you're like me, you quickly blame others and your circumstances for your problems instead of looking at your heart. I struggle to humble myself to other people. I struggle to admit when I have sinned against God and others. I struggle to submit to His word and address my heart genuinely. It usually takes a few "stop signs" and "traffic lights" for me to turn back to His perfect ways.

How have you been driving? The beautiful truth is that "God gives more grace." He does resist the proud heart, but He will pour His grace if you humble yourself!

Question: What should I do when I'm not walking in the Spirit?

Answer: Slow down, low down, lay down, and turn around.

Bible Passages for Further Study

- Colossians 3
- 1 Thessalonians 5
- Ephesians 5:18–19
- Psalm 51; 32

Discussion Questions

1. What circumstances make it difficult for you to yield to the Holy Spirit?

2. What steps could you take to reconcile with another person?

3. What activities or loves make humility and repentance challenging for you?

4. What steps could you take each day to build habits of correct response?

5. How could you help others respond well in sanctification?

REFLECT

BEHOLDING AND DEMONSTRATING THE GLORY OF GOD

Question 10

What Happens When I Respond to Trials the Correct Way?

As we saw in section 1, God's will, first, involves an internal change. His will begins with salvation and continues through sanctification. While we live here on earth, God accomplishes our sanctification by allowing trials. These trials cultivate our transformation by revealing internal areas of idolatry or immorality that God desires to change.

Then in section 2, we considered how our response during trials should include the Holy Spirit. We "walk in the Spirit" when we are under His control and manifest His fruits both internally and externally. Walking in the Spirit is not an emotion forced upon us by an outside influence. In fact, we often have conflicting emotions as we struggle to yield to the Holy Spirit's control and obey God's Word. When we are walking in the Spirit, we obey God's Word with proper and changing motivations. Even with mixed motivations and desires, we yield and turn to the desires of the Spirit rather than the flesh.

Why?

In this third section, we aim to answer the question why: Why respond correctly during trials? First, each of us receives spiritual fruit from correct responses. Our genuine repentance and communion with God's Spirit allow the Holy Spirit to give us these fruits. And who does not want love, joy, and peace?

Another answer to why believers should seek a correct response comes from Paul in 2 Corinthians. In this letter Paul describes his reasoning and motivation for seeking to minister well through trials. The rest of this chapter examines Paul's ministry philosophy to answer why believers should strive to live controlled by the Spirit.

Paul's Ministry Philosophy

In 2 Corinthians 2, Paul describes how spiritual transformation produces the "aroma of Christ." In chapter 4, he further describes transformation as a great light, "the glory of God." Sanctification, therefore, produces a scent and a light: as we become more like Jesus, God's glory is reflected, and others see and "smell" Jesus. Paul considered this production of Christ's aroma and God's glory inseparable from his ministry.

We Christians speak about "doing all to the glory of God," but many pursue personal ease instead of devoted humility and walking in the Spirit. Similarly, some ministries quickly train converts to share the bullet points of the gospel without devoting effort to cultivate fruitfulness in personal sanctification. God loves you, regardless of who you are, but God wants to change you so that you reflect His perfect character in a dark, dying world. Discipleship, or any form of ministry, devoid of the transforming power of the Holy Spirit in sanctification would have confounded Paul. He knew he had nothing to offer on his own without the work of God in his sanctification.

As we answer what happens when we respond to trials correctly, we will consider five facets of Paul's ministry philosophy regarding sanctification and the glory of God. The remainder of this chapter is a brief overview of a vibrant section of Scripture, 2 Corinthians 2—4. We will not cover every detail, so I recommend reading this section thoroughly on your own. We will see from Paul that we do not have genuine discipleship without sanctification.

Sanctification Opens Doors

Imagine that a missionary visits your church this Sunday and shares about recent ministry experiences. As is customary, the missionary shows a map of the area, describes the abundant need related to the number of unreached people, and clicks through a few pictures of recent opportunities. Then the missionary says, "We had so many open doors for ministry, but we decided to leave!" Does your internal voice question that decision? It seems a bit counterintuitive, right? Why would anyone leave open doors behind? In 2 Corinthians 2, Paul explains how he made that same decision: he left open doors behind! Why would Paul do this?

Paul mentions in 2:12 that he had an open door of ministry but *left it* to seek Titus in Macedonia. On a practical level, Paul sought Titus to learn valuable information regarding the work and ministry in Corinth. Regardless of the specific reason, Paul knew that his ministry continued in every location (even after leaving open opportunity behind).

Paul understood that personal sanctification produces results regardless of geographical location. Paul therefore praises God for Christ's leading him in ministry (2:14), for Christ led Paul and the apostles into successful ministry wherever they traveled.

Is successful ministry a certain number of converts, or is it disciples' follow-through to obey? Is successful ministry the result of some ratio of open doors to tangible standards? Providentially, *Paul set the mark of ministry success: success is the presence of transformation.* Even if an unbeliever rejects the gospel message, a ministry succeeds if the rejection follows a simple proclamation of truth from a believer with genuine character. To recap, Paul's ministry philosophy defined success as the character of Christ displayed to others through personal sanctification.

If we possess the glory of Christ, we can come and go as we please. Ministry will happen wherever the glory of God presents itself through our sanctification. Lasting discipleship will produce open doors; we do not need to strive after them.

 Ministry will happen wherever the glory of God presents itself through our sanctification. Lasting discipleship will produce open doors; we do not need to strive after them.

Sanctification Diffuses an Aroma

Drawing from the historical imagery of a Roman victory parade, Paul described the second facet of ministry success with a smell. A victorious Roman general would march through a city, leading his army and any captives. Such a march was a celebration, a parade of glory. People would fill the streets, gather to watch, and shout. As in modern parades, specific smells accompanied the victory parade, including the smell of burning incense. Quite literally, victory had a smell.

In Paul's example (2 Cor 2:14–16), Christ is the victorious general who conquered death and the grave. His captives believe and receive victory by His grace and mercy. Therefore, the victorious smell of Christ accompanied Paul and his companions wherever they traveled. Paul describes their smell as "the aroma of Christ to God among those . . . who are perishing." Even today, the victory smell of Christ travels all over the world as faithful believers carry His aroma.

Paul indicates here that people *would smell* who Christ is the closer they got to Paul. The aroma of Christ drew some to life and others to death, but Paul considered his efforts successful based on having the smell and not on anyone's response to the scent. So, the minister of the gospel smells good, other people smell the scent of Christ, and that aroma stimulates responses.

Successful ministry, therefore, "smells like Christ." How "stinky" are you? The *aroma of Christ* will draw some people to life and others to death. This aroma results from the character, conduct, and conversation of a transformed life. God allows tests and trials that direct us to internal struggles. If we repent and humble ourselves, God graciously produces the aroma of His Son. Thus, successful ministry results from internal transformation.

Notice the question Paul asks in 2 Corinthians 2:16, "Who is sufficient for these things?" (ESV). I can relate. I am unable to perform many tasks or jobs. For example, I will never be a professional athlete, because I'm not fit, strong, or fast enough. If I wanted a profession like doctor, lawyer, engineer, I would need a lot of education first; I am currently unequipped for any of those jobs. Can you relate? What jobs are you insufficient to accomplish?

When it comes to diffusing the aroma of Christ, Paul says that nobody is sufficient. None of us can do ministry on our own, because none of us produce the aroma of Christ on our own. God, however, facilitates sufficiency through our trials, training, and transformation.

Furthermore, the person whom God makes sufficient is sufficient. Without God's help and presence none of us do ministry. And this is the answer. What happens when I respond correctly? Ministry happens. God produces the aroma of Christ in us. People smell us, but in a good way! Why should we seek to yield, humble ourselves, submit, and repent? Because correct responses in trial bring sufficiency. So, the most relevant ministry strategy is sanctification.

Sanctification Reflects Glory

Paul switches the metaphor from smell to light as he further describes ministry sufficiency in 2 Corinthians. He builds an argument from lesser to greater, explaining how the glory, or light, produced by the Holy Spirit in the hearts of believers far surpasses the old covenant glory. The old covenant, described as "the ministry of death engraved on stones," and the "ministry of condemnation" refers to the Old Testament law. Paul's epistles to the Galatians and Romans teach that the law reveals and magnifies sin but cannot produce righteousness. People who try to follow the law should realize their inability to earn righteousness before a holy God. Paul's summary to the Romans is fitting: "There are none righteous, no not one." Recognizing sinfulness through the law points people to a need for a savior to redeem and deliver them.

The gospel accomplishes much more than the law does, for the law reveals unrighteousness, but the gospel brings righteousness. When we trust Jesus to forgive sin, God declares us righteous based on Jesus Christ's perfection and holiness. Once we are saved, more righteousness comes through our submission to the Holy Spirit, not through law keeping. Sanctification results in the glorious light of Christ's character that God produces in us as we walk in the Spirit.

Paul's illustration of light mirrors the Old Testament account of Moses. When Moses received the law in the wilderness, God produced light. The record in Exodus 34 emphasizes how Moses's face was *literally glowing or shining* from his being in God's presence. In short, time spent in the presence of God or communing with God produces light. When believers spend time in God's presence, they reflect His light. So, the light of Christ reflects through transformed lives.

Believe the Gospel

The first production of Christ's light becomes evident in someone's life when that person believes the gospel. Borrowing from the veil terminology in Exodus, Paul paints a picture of the spiritual condition of humanity. All people have a "veil" over their hearts, including people who try to read the Old Testament law and earn righteousness apart from faith. Just as Moses put a literal veil over his shining face to keep people from seeing the glory, all people are born with a figurative veil over the eyes of their hearts. In other words, all are born in sin and naturally suppress the truth of the gospel as God's enemies.

Belief in the gospel, however, cures spiritual blindness, even though many people still attempt to earn righteousness through law keeping or righteous effort. Galatians says, "If righteousness could be earned through the law, Christ died in vain" (2:21). According to 2 Corinthians 3:16, only turning to the Lord (Jesus) removes the veil. Removing the veil illustrates salvation: we have a veil on our hearts, keeping us from seeing Christ; but if we believe the gospel, He removes the veil and transforms us. He makes us new creatures, as Paul states later in his ministry philosophy (2 Cor 5).

Behold the Glory

We can see sanctification in the chronology of Paul's metaphor. In 2 Corinthians 3:14, Christ—who is directly named—removes the veil. In verse 16, Christ, called Lord, removes the veil when someone turns to Him in belief. Verse 17 uses the same title, Lord, but there Paul does not use the title to refer to Jesus. Instead, the word *Spirit* is used three times in verses 17 and 18. Why would Paul distinguish between Christ as Lord in 2 Corinthians 3:14–16 and the Holy Spirit as Lord in 2 Corinthians 3:17–18?

Remember: progressive sanctification depends on a correct response to the Holy Spirit, who indwells us. Look closely at the wording of verse 18; "unveiled face" refers to our salvation. Christ removed the veil. Unlike unbelievers, believers have unrestricted communion with God within the heart and in God's Word. Born-again believers receive the Holy Spirit to guide them into truth. We have a new capacity to "behold the glory of God" in the Word of God, which transforms us into the same image. Moses spent time with the Lord, and his face shined. Believers today get much more than a facelift from spending time with God; we get a heart transplant that affects our whole lives.

> Believers today get much more than a facelift from spending time with God; we get a heart transplant that affects our whole lives.

Sanctification Combats Opposition

God's adversary, "the god of this world," wants spiritually blind people to remain blind, so he actively tries to veil the gospel's message and keep people from seeing the glory of God. The adversary knows that "the light of the gospel of the glory of Christ" may lead some to salvation. Though people's natural, sinful condition hinders them from understanding the gospel, the adversary knows that if they behold the glory of God, it is a problem for him.

What does God do to combat the adversary's attempts? Verses 5 and 6 explain: "God who commanded light to shine out of darkness has shown in our hearts to give the light of the knowledge of the glory of God in the face of Jesus Christ." *The same God who created light at the universe's founding creates light in us believers through our transformation (2 Cor 3:18). God draws people to Himself using discipleship. Growing disciples make other disciples.*

Whether it is our scent or our light, God's work in our hearts leads some people to life and others to death. While the adversary wants to keep people from seeing that aroma and light, God desires to reflect light and diffuse the aroma of Christ through us. So, Paul gave off the aroma of Christ and reflected Christ everywhere he went. Likewise, we diffuse Christ's aroma and reflect Christ's light everywhere we go. When we have the aroma and the light of Christ—if we choose to suffer correctly—ministry will take place.

> When we have the aroma and the light of Christ—if we choose to suffer correctly—ministry will take place.

Sanctification Prioritizes Suffering

If you've been a Christian long enough, you have heard some-one mention living "for the glory of God." What does it mean to glorify God? There is value in recognizing God's preeminence in everything we do and recognizing that "whether we eat, or drink, or whatever we do," we operate for God's glory. However, 2 Cor-inthians 2—4 should change how we think about bringing God glory. Glorifying God is not an empty ritual. In fact, in our progres-sive sanctification, we *manifest* God's glory or "make it evident by showing or displaying" it. We are responsible for sanctification daily so the Holy Spirit may produce God's glory in us. As Paul knew, suffering helps produce the glory of God. Therefore, if we genuinely seek to do everything "for God's glory," we must learn to suffer well.

Paul completed his picture of light by comparing believers to an empty pot, specifically, an earthen vessel or clay pot. So, the physical body is a worthless container; nothing about our bodies is uniquely profound. We may, however, possess a valuable treasure *in the vessel*: as vessels, we are light bearers or aroma diffusers of God's glory. We exist to carry this treasure before God and to oth-ers. God's will is to produce this treasure in our vessels so the blind will see or smell Christ.

"Giving glory to God" means much more than uttering His name after a big play or posting a morning Bible reading on social me-dia. Most people hate pain, but to glorify God, believers learn to embrace it. Cultivating correct love in the heart is difficult, requires self-denial, and lacks the glamour sought in our modern culture. Genuine discipleship is off brand. The heavy lifting of sanctification requires a mind and heart resolute on enduring difficulty for no other reason than God's glory.

Cultivating correct love in the heart is difficult, requires self-denial, and lacks the glamour sought in our modern culture. Genuine discipleship is off brand.

According to 2 Corinthians 4:12, believers must embrace pain in sanctification: "Death is at work in us, but life in you" (ESV). The death Paul mentioned broadly refers to the presence of severe trials experienced by his ministry partners and him. As we have learned, those trials were a means by which God humbled Paul and transformed him. And once he was transformed, the aroma and light of Christ reflected from him. The glory of Christ in Paul extended beyond him and affected the people he ministered to; therefore, God used *death* in Paul's life to produce life in the Corinthians! This philosophy of ministry applies to evangelism, teaching, preaching, and any other form of discipleship. Any ministry we are privileged to perform extends God's glory through His transforming work in our trials.

Any ministry we are privileged to perform extends God's glory through His transforming work in our trials.

This chapter asks, What happens when I respond to trials the correct way? The answer is *ministry. God's glory extends to other people.* Because it's easy to manipulate people in fleshly ways, we can easily win people through personality, community, social gatherings, and the like. But authentic discipleship happens when the presence of God's Spirit transforms others through the reflection of Christ's glory, which starts in our own hearts. The Holy Spirit produces the great treasure of the aroma and light of Christ, and that treasure leads other people to Him. We minister the gospel of Christ to others through our consistent response of humility and repentance amid trials.

Question: What happens when I respond to trials the correct way?

Answer: Ministry, as God's glory is produced and extends to others.

Bible Passages for Further Study

- 2 Corinthians 1—7 (Spend a bunch of time here.)

Discussion Questions

1. What two metaphors does Paul use in 2 Corinthians 2—4 to illustrate successful ministry?

2. Who accomplishes transformation (2 Cor 3:18)?

3. What was Paul's confidence in ministry (2 Cor 3:4)?

4. Where does Paul draw "boldness" from according to 2 Corinthians 3:12?

5. How does the production of God's glory through the Holy Spirit affect the way we should pursue discipleship ministry?

What Kind of Vessel Am I?

In chapter 10, we answered the question, What happens when I respond to trials the correct way? We saw in Scripture that ministry happens as God's glory is produced and extends to others.

We learned that Paul's ministry philosophy can direct our discipleship aspirations and goals: the transformation of the Holy Spirit (2 Cor 3:18), producing the glory of Christ, should be the focus in any ministry and all discipleship. Ministry begins in the heart, engaging the daily process of sanctification. Next, we disciples develop patterns that allow the Holy Spirit to transform our hearts. Internal and external transformation then makes us personally sufficient to go forward and assist others in their transformation.

Treasure the Treasure, Not the Vessel

In his other letters, Paul built upon the vessel picture from 2 Corinthians 4:7. Specifically, 2 Timothy 2:20–21 employs the same term for vessel that Paul employed in 2 Corinthians 4:7. Paul wanted Timothy to view the lives of the Ephesian believers (whom Timothy was likely pastoring) as vessels or containers because vessels illustrate the character and preparation of believers who pursue ministry or discipleship.

Paul compared two kinds of vessels: cleansed and uncleansed. He was reminding Timothy that Timothy's goal for evangelizing and discipling in Ephesus was for him to be a cleansed vessel and for him to influence other cleansed vessels.

How Clean Are the Dishes?

During this illustration of vessels, Paul describes a house, so imagine your house. Think about all the kinds of containers in your house and the tasks they help accomplish. Most houses have cups, bowls, plates, and more for eating and drinking, which are probably stored in the kitchen area. My mom, for example, owns different kinds of containers for various occasions, and some of them are more valuable than others due to their quality.

Paul reminded Timothy that different types of vessels serve in various tasks: vessels for simple tasks and vessels for important tasks; vessels made of gold and silver and vessels made of clay.

Does clay pot sound familiar?

We believers know we are clay pots, not possessing ministry sufficiency on our own. Sufficiency is independent of a vessel's value but, rather, depends on the value of the treasure inside. Being a clay pot is fine; further, a broken clay pot accentuates the glory and value of the treasure inside it. We believers are not vessels made of gold or silver, but that is okay, because ministry success hinges on our (the vessels') contents, not on our inherent quality.

The characteristic required for a "vessel" to be ready for the Master's use is internal cleansing. Passages like Deuteronomy 8, James 1, and Jamess 4 anticipate this internal cleansing of the heart. In the process of sanctification and yielding to the Spirit's control, repentance cleanses a believer from the influence of the flesh. Our internal cleansing includes our walking in the Spirit and being filled by the Spirit. Trials, therefore, become cleansing agents in sanctification.

The effectiveness of Paul's "vessel-ology" persists today because everybody understands this picture! Customary hospitality entails offering guests a drink: "Would you like a glass of water? Great! One moment. Here you go!" How skeptical would you be if I brought that glass of water from the bathroom instead of the kitchen? "How about we wash that cup a few hundred times first?" you might think. You probably wouldn't be thinking, "Who cares what you used the cup for last time? I'm sure it's clean!"

In ancient times, people filled clay pots with some horrendous things. I'll encourage you to study that fact on your own, but here's a hint: some vessels still get used this way today but are often porcelain.

 In short, we are insufficient for ministry if we are not cleansed from the flesh and yielded to Christ. How we respond during a trial demonstrates whether our spiritual influence contains the purity of the Spirit or the contamination of the flesh.

Just as we are selective about the vessels we drink and eat from, so the Master uses only cleansed vessels. In short, we are insufficient for ministry if we are not cleansed from the flesh and yielded to Christ. How we respond during a trial demonstrates whether our spiritual influence contains the purity of the Spirit or the contamination of the flesh. Natural, fleshly reactions infect us and affect the people around us. If we resist cleansing and allow the flesh to remain in control, we might still give off an aroma, but the flesh does not smell like Christ. If we perform all the external tasks and jump over every physical hurdle but fleshy desires motivate us, we have avoided the true hurdles within the heart. An uncleaned vessel is useless and inactive because that believer lacks Holy Spirit control and cleansing.

Rinse and Repeat

Please do not misunderstand. Disciples and disciple-makers do not need perfection, and we should not fear failure. Obedience to God's Word and His ways always involves some element of mixed desires; we will never escape the presence of our flesh in this life.

According to Galatians 5, the internal work of the Spirit wars and fights against the flesh. The point is not to reach a certain level of sanctification where fleshly impulses are gone; rather, we need awareness and training in humility and submission. We must not become pridefully unaware of the need to confess sin and be humble with others.

> The point is not to reach a certain level of sanctification where fleshly impulses are gone; rather, we need awareness and training in humility and submission. We must not become pridefully unaware of the need to confess sin and be humble with others.

Many people pridefully resist admitting when they're wrong. All of us believers struggle to confess sin to one another, but transformation comes when we see sin at work within ourselves and we humble ourselves to the Holy Spirit's work. We must turn to God and be cleansed; His grace transforms. So, humility as a response unlocks the door of sanctification. Humility and cleansing are paramount to our becoming ready, serviceable vessels. Without cleansing, we are not prepared.

As we consider the task of discipleship, we should seek to present ourselves daily for cleansing by the Master. For example, even if I don't think I've done anything wrong or sinful, I want to devote time to prayer and meditation to present my heart to God for washing and cleansing through His Word—this is the most vital and most challenging task of discipleship.

I easily live on autopilot and avoid proper internal recognition and cleansing. I'm tempted to believe and think cleansing doesn't impact my ministry, but God's Word says it does. If I neglect the responsibility of being a cleansed vessel, my ministry reeks of self-effort. The last thing I want to find out at the end of my life is that I labored through fleshly means of self-effort.

Therefore, as ministers of the gospel, we must commit to daily cleansing. In our moments of devotion, we should pour our hearts before the Lord and ask Him to make us sufficient as gospel ministers and to cleanse us so we are vessels ready for His use. We want the Holy Spirit to move through us and freely extend to others around us. Unclean vessels will cease to possess the work and fruit of the Spirit; the glory will not extend through us to others around us.

 The best days of ministry are rarely days without the need to yield or repent but, rather, are days filled with frequent prayer and crying out for grace and mercy in moments of need.

What amazes me is how quickly all this can change. The moment we yield to the Spirit, He works within us. Never give yourself the benefit of the doubt. Instead, be quick each day to repent and present yourself before God for cleansing. *The best days of ministry are rarely days without the need to yield or repent but, rather, are days filled with frequent prayer and crying out for grace and mercy in moments of need.* Remember, "God gives more grace."

What kind of vessel are you? From 2 Timothy 2:20–21, understand that we are either cleansed and ready vessels or uncleansed vessels unprepared for use. Examine your heart. Is the presence of the flesh defiling the inside you? Spend time evaluating what kind of vessel you are and take the necessary steps of internal cleansing. Communing with the Holy Spirit leads to transformation. Your communion with God's Spirit (2 Cor 3:18) fills your vessel with the treasure. Let the Spirit do His work.

Question: What kind of vessel am I?

Answer: Cleansed and ready or uncleansed and unused.

Bible Passages for Further Study

- 2 Timothy 2:20–21
- 1 Thessalonians 4:1–8
- Matthew 23:25–28
- Psalm 51

Discussion Questions

1. Why is it important for you to cleanse the inside of your vessel?

2. What kinds of sins defile you most often?

3. What keeps you from being cleansed?

4. How does an uncleansed vessel hinder discipleship?

5. How can you help others stay cleansed?

Do People See Christ in Me?

In this section we have asked, What happens when I respond to trials the right way? and found the answer: Ministry happens as God's glory is produced and extends to others. We also considered what kind of vessels we are and learned that we can be either cleansed and ready for use by God or uncleansed and unused.

Review

This chapter is the culmination of a long series of questions. We started broadly, asking, "What is God's will?" God's will is to transform us by using pressure through tests and trials. We learned that moments of spiritual training increase our awareness of the powers at work in our hearts (loves, motives, desires, etc.). And we considered how God allows difficult people, circumstances, and temptations to train us to respond to Him in humility and trust.

We also considered how a correct response prioritizes control by the Holy Spirit over the control by the flesh. Trials and tests are moments when the flesh naturally reacts and seeks control. But when trials restrict our desires and we submit to God's Spirit, transformation takes place. God trains us believers to yield to the Holy Spirit, humble ourselves, submit to His Word, and live repentant lives. Trials teach us to stop straining with the flesh and turn to Christ.

In this last section, we are studying the results of humility and submission. Through humility and submission, we disciples allow the Spirit to produce the distinct aroma and glorious light of Christ in us. God transforms us to be like Christ when we correctly respond to spiritual training. Therefore, trials have the potential to produce the glorious character of God in us. And believers who are being transformed reflect the power of God to other people. This reflection of God's glory takes place through progressive sanctification.

One Last Question

Recap

Armed with eleven answers, readers should find this twelfth question simple. But keep in mind, simple does not mean easy. Today have you responded in a way that allows the Holy Spirit to produce the aroma and light of Christ in you? What actions or words require repentance? What loves, motives, and desires need cleansing? "Draw near to the Lord, and he will draw near to you."

Thankfully, the results are up to someone else. If they were up to us, we would be manufacturers or manipulators instead of disciples and disciple-makers. Yes, we own the task of faithful service to God, the ministry of beholding and bearing a treasure in earthly vessels. Yes, we strive to walk in the Spirit, turning from the gratifying desires of the flesh and seeking to bear the spiritual fruit of righteousness to a dark world. But it is the Holy Spirit who draws people to the heavenly Father through Christ's character in us.

> But it is the Holy Spirit who draws people to the heavenly Father through Christ's character in us.

My Response

Do other people see fruit in your life? Many days, my initial answer is no. Too often I search my heart and see my brokenness, count my failures, and resist God's work in my heart. I recognize, sometimes quickly but other times much delayed, the influence and control of my flesh. Thankfully, one prayer of repentance allows the cleansing and communion my soul needs. Repentance and humility quench the thirst of my heart as it searches for water in a dry land. Days full of failure then become great days of ministry and discipleship. God uses our failures. But I must ask, Am I willing to humble myself?

Some days, I neglect to yield to the Holy Spirit. From an outsider's perspective, these days seem perfectly normal. I may have done everything right externally, but I was powering through my day on self-effort. To accomplish the task of discipleship, I need days controlled by the Holy Spirit. When I humble myself to the Spirit, I allow the production and reflection of the aroma and light of Christ. Those are the truly successful days.

What could cap this book would be a heartwarming story about how someone saw Christ in another believer; it led that person to the Lord; and, you guessed it, the rest is history! I do have such stories. I saw the glory of Christ in others, and that light led me to salvation. I have smelled the aroma of Christ in others, and that smell helped me grow and draw closer to the Lord. Ask your pastor or friends, and they'll tell you stories too. Our churches are full of tales of how love, joy, peace, patience, kindness, goodness, faithfulness, gentleness, and self-control in a faithful disciple guided people further up and further into the Christian faith.

Do people see Christ in me? That is my aim, for God's glory. I want the words of my mouth and the meditations of my heart to be pleasing to God and used by God in the lives of others.

 Do people see Christ in you?

And You?

Do people see Christ in you? That is a good question. If your answer is no, recognize what is at work in your heart, respond by yielding control to the Holy Spirit, and reflect Christ's character. If you learn and continue to walk in the Spirit, you cannot mess it up.

Conclusion

After completing the twelve discipleship questions, let's return to the first questions in the introduction: What makes a good definition of discipleship, and by what standard should we measure success?

Successful discipleship involves recognition. Spiritual recognition begins with understanding God's will of internal transformation, or sanctification, for each disciple. Further spiritual awareness consists in knowing how God uses tests and trials to reveal the loves, motives, and desires at work in our hearts. With increased recognition of the heart, we disciples focus on responding correctly.

1. Successful discipleship involves response. We learn to obey the warnings of God's Word. And as we fear the Lord, we begin to gain wisdom. Wisdom, in turn, leads to a correct response to trials, which includes understanding the loves, motives, and desires that influence and control our obedience or disobedience. Trials, furthermore, provide opportunities for walking in the Spirit and being filled by the Spirit. The fruits of the Spirit—love, joy, peace, etc.—are not treasures found on some mystical journey or purchased with productivity; rather, these virtuous fruits grow from transformed roots in our hearts. The Holy Spirit bears fruit in any believer who yields, humbles, submits, and repents.

2. Successful discipleship involves our reflection of God's character to others. While personal transformation flows from recognition and response, it results in reflection. As transformed, sanctified believers, we serve the Lord by diffusing knowledge of Christ as an aroma and by reflecting the glory of Christ. This treasure shines from within clean vessels.

Final Encouragements

Of course, discipleship means many more things too. Consider these twelve questions as a template, a map that begins the discipleship journey. God works to sanctify each believer in Christ. If you've tracked along, you know exactly how God does his work. When we humble ourselves, God gives us grace. Additionally, the longer we are engaged in this process, the more we should seek to lead others. Our closest friends should be believers who challenge us with these truths, and we should challenge them right back! Mature Christians never outgrow the need for character transformation before heaven.

The Lord willing, you will begin to apply these questions and will seek to disciple others, making maturity and discipleship lifelong pursuits. Spiritual training is not a project to complete in a few weeks or months. Spiritual training takes baby steps, but those small daily steps add up over a lifetime. You will look back a year or two or ten from now and realize that you are not the same person you were. Hopefully, you and many others will see you become more like Christ.

Think of these lessons from Scripture. When the shepherd leaves the ninety-nine sheep to find the one, he rejoices after finding his lost sheep. When the woman finds her lost coin, she rejoices. When the prodigal son returns, the father meets him before he reaches home to rejoice that he has returned. Likewise, when you respond to trials in humility, confess to God the work of your flesh, and seek to commune with Him through the Holy Spirit and the

Word, God meets and rejoices with you. May your life and ministry be filled with joy as God and His Spirit control you. May your discipleship road go on and on.

FAQs

Many practical questions regarding discipleship were not answered in this book, but here are a few quick thoughts just so I can get them on a page:

How often should people meet for discipleship?

There is no wrong answer. Word to the wise: if you plan to meet every week, you will likely end up meeting every other week. If you plan to meet every other week, don't be surprised when you end up meeting once a month. If you plan to meet once a month, well . . . you get the idea. People make time for what they deem important.

How long does it take for someone to mature?

When I first gained interest in discipleship ministry, I asked my pastor this question. His answer: "Oh . . . two to ten years. And some make it four or five pretty well, then turn away." I thought he was crazy. No way those numbers were correct. But he was right.

Is one-on-one discipleship better than small groups?

Some conversations will only happen one-on-one, but other conversations will only happen with three or more. Sometimes creativity about the person you meet with and the time you meet stimulates disciples to take necessary steps. That being said, you build trust the fastest when you're forced to sit in silence with one other person.

How many people should I disciple?

Be a good steward. If you're married, focus on your family first. If you're unmarried, be selfless with your time. Ask yourself what you can realistically do with excellence. If that is one or ninety-nine, go and make disciples!

How do I know if I'm ready to disciple another?

Ask your pastor. Ask the one discipling you or a close friend or mentor. Ask your spouse. Listen to the wise people around you. If you have a consistent pattern of responding correctly to trials and your spiritual influence reflects the fruits of the Holy Spirit, you might be ready. God knows, just trust Him.

www.ingramcontent.com/pod-product-compliance
Lightning Source LLC
Chambersburg PA
CBHW022020210125
20607CB00048B/1094